RECLAIMING
DEMOCRACY

RECLAIMING DEMOCRACY

THE SIXTIES IN POLITICS AND MEMORY

Meta Mendel-Reyes

Routledge New York & London

Published in 1995 by
Routledge
29 West 35th Street
New York, NY 10001

Published in Great Britain by
Routledge
11 New Fetter Lane
London EC4P 4EE

A portion of the Preface has been previously published as "Remembering Cesar," in *Radical History Review* no. 58, 1994.

Design: David Thorne
Printed in the United States of America on acid-free paper.

Library of Congress Cataloging-in-Publication Data
Mendel-Reyes, Meta.
   Reclaiming democracy: the Sixties in politics and memory / Meta Mendel-Reyes.
   p.   cm.
   Includes bibliographical references and index.
   ISBN 0-415-91134-6 (hb: acid-free paper)
   1. Political participation—United States—History—20th century.   2. Social movements—United States—History—20th century.   3. United States—Politics and government—1963–1969.   4. United States—Social conditions—1960–1980.
   I. Title.

JK1764.M46   1995   95-700
323'.042'0973—dc20   CIP

To the two Jackies:

my mother, Jacqueline Kramer Mendel
1919–1972

and my daughter, Jacqueline Mendel-Reyes
1981–

CONTENTS

ACKNOWLEDGMENTS

According to an African proverb, "It takes a village to raise a child." In my experience, this is also true of writing a book and of living a life. I would like to acknowledge the help and support that I have received from the people of my "village," which now stretches from Pennsylvania to the Philippines, with a stopover in California. There is no way to rank your gifts, so I hope that you will not mind being listed in alphabetical order: Adam Bohannon; Victoria Brennan; Aurora Camacho de Schmidt; Cecelia Cancellaro; Cesar Chavez; Kate Cleland; Nadinne Cruz; Mona D'Astarte; J. Peter Euben; Debbie Fisher; Todd Gitlin; Claudia Gorelick; Cynthia Halpern; Raymond Hopkins; Judith Howard; Norman Jacobson; Terry Johnston; Shithi Kamal; Kathleen Kerns; Kevin Keenan; James Kurth; Faith Lindsay; Ngina Lythcott; Rina Margolin; Zulene Mayfield; Jacqueline Kramer Mendel; Rob Mendel; Robin Mendel Montoya; Marjorie Murphy; Carol Nackenoff; June Oberdorfer; Deepa Ollapally; Emeliza Olimpo; Hanna Fenichel Pitkin; Niko Pfund; Jacqueline Mendel-Reyes; Rodolfo Reyes; Michael Paul Rogin; Henry Tom; John Schaar; Kenneth Sharpe; Debbie Sloman; Russell Stark; Nanette Tobin; Peggy Thompson;

Ellen Kay Trimberger; Joan Tronto; Richard Valelly; Jacob Weiner; Tyrene White; Graham Wilson; Sheldon Wolin; and anonymous reviewers from Routledge and Princeton University Press.

I would also like to acknowledge the following organizations and programs: the American Friends Service Committee National Women's Program and the working group on Women, Poverty, and Economic Power; Chester Residents Concerned for Quality Living; Chester Community Improvement Project; CIVIC, Swarthmore College; the Committee Against Xenophobia, Swarthmore College; the Communications Workers of America, AFL-CIO; the Democracy Project of the Department of Political Science, Swarthmore College; the Department of Political Science, University of California at Berkeley; the Invisible College, sponsored by Campus Compact; Routledge; the 1993 Leo Strauss Award Committee of the American Political Science Association; the students in PS 1, 17, 19, and 38, during 1994–95; the United Farm Workers Union, AFL-CIO; the Service Employees International Union, AFL-CIO, Locals 535 and 715.

I am grateful for financial support from the Swarthmore College Research Fund.

Lastly, I would like to acknowledge Penny, who left her pawprint on nearly every page of the manuscript.

PREFACE

"THE THREAD OF HOPEFUL MEMORY"

The Sixties made a difference....
I have wanted to keep the thread
of hopeful memory alive.

—John Schaar, *Legitimacy in the*
Modern State

ON the day after the historic
Republican triumph in the 1994
midterm elections, Newt
Gingrich, about to become the
next Speaker of the House,
announced the theme for the
first GOP-controlled Congress
in forty years: "There are
profound things that went
wrong with the Great Society

and the counterculture and until we address them head-on, we're going to have these problems." He predicted a ten- to twelve-year battle against "liberal elites," to put the country back on the right track:

> Until the mid-1960s, there was an explicit longterm commitment to creating character. It was the work ethic. It was honesty, right and wrong. It was not harming others. It was being vigilant in the defense of liberty.[1]

If the sixties stand for immorality, laziness, dishonesty, and violence, then no wonder Gingrich claims that, as the *New York Times* emphasized in a large subheading, "America wants to undo the legacy of the 60s."[2] Gingrich's declaration of war against the decade is the latest attempt to reunify the American people on the basis of a highly selective memory of the sixties. What has been left out is the surge in political participation by ordinary Americans, in the civil rights movement, the New Left, and the early women's liberation movement.

The politics of the nineties have been organized, to a much greater extent than most Americans realize, around the question of who owns the sixties. The electoral victory celebrated by Gingrich solidified the dominant, negative interpretation, which condemns the sixties movements as undemocratic, while trying to erase all traces of the positive experience of participatory politics. Its success is indicated by my publisher's relief that I had decided, for independent reasons, to remove the sixties slogan, "participatory democracy," from the title of this book. Later, the marketing department removed the phrase from the catalog copy, explaining to me that it could hurt the book's sales.

Yet, these two words, so out of favor, simply express the most direct way in which each of us can have a say in the life of the community. The basic meaning of democracy is the rule of the people. Only when everyone participates in making and carrying out political decisions can we be sure that the people do, in fact, rule. Of course, the questions of how and to what extent full participation can be achieved are challenging, but throughout American history, some of our best thinkers and activists have taken them on. Why is the mere memory of this country's latest experiment in participatory democracy on a large scale so threatening today? Of course, the few who benefit from the apathy of the many may want to hide the history of participatory politics, but why haven't the sixties movements inspired those who suffer the most from the present, unequal distribution of power and resources?

My sense that the democratic story of the sixties is worth reclaiming comes, in part, from personal experience. Over twenty years ago, the civil rights movement inspired me to participate in politics. I graduated from college in 1972, too young to have gone to Mississippi during Freedom Summer. But the memory of Southern blacks and Northern students working together for justice and interracial democracy encouraged me, in 1974, to join another such movement, the United Farm Workers, led by Cesar Chavez. The UFW was the first labor organization to be founded and run by the farmworkers themselves, mostly Mexicans, but also Filipinos, Arabs, African Americans, and whites.[3] They adapted the nonviolent tactics of the civil rights movement to improve working conditions that had barely changed since the nineteenth century: child labor, lack of access to drinking water and toilets, ten- and twelve-hour days, no minimum wage. Four years as a full-time volunteer with the UFW, followed by another ten years in labor organizing, showed me both the promise and the challenge of participatory politics.

One of my favorite memories of Cesar Chavez reveals a less well-known side of the charismatic farmworker leader. He struts at the back of a noisy, crowded meeting, presided over (barely) by four beleaguered farmworkers seated around a table in front. As this ranch committee struggles through its first attempt at parliamentary procedure, Cesar pulls a comb out of his back pocket and elaborately combs his hair. The contrast between this study in self-absorption and the saintly image of the leader of *La Causa* finally causes me to burst out laughing, along with nearly everyone else in the hall, even the frustrated group at the front. Cesar grins, puts the comb back in his pocket, and walks toward the stage, where he leads a discussion about this class exercise in running a meeting.

It's 1975, not long after the California Agricultural Labor Relations Act has been passed, and the mostly Mexican farmworkers are faced with the challenge of learning how to exercise the power they struggled so long to attain. So, here we are, farmworker organizers from all over the state along with a handful of full-time volunteers like me, teaching ourselves the skills of democracy. As our leader, Cesar is right here among us, modeling an approach to leadership in which everyone becomes a leader.

Flash forward to 1978, the same meeting hall, hot and crowded, but not noisy. Cesar presides from behind a podium, and the audience, many of the same people, listen quietly to his report of his trip to the Philippines. A few of us are troubled. How could Cesar allow himself to be the guest of the dictator Ferdinand Marcos, who stands for everything we're fighting against? Although I know the answer, that Cesar went to the Philippines in an attempt to win the votes of Filipino workers in representational elections, I'm still concerned.

Finally, during the question-and-answer period, I raise the issue, nervously. Cesar says something brief and evasive, accompanied by his reassuring smile. Immediately, another organizer leaps to his feet, proclaiming that whatever Cesar does is all right by him. Pointing to the white wall behind him, he shouts, "If Cesar said that wall was black, so would I!" Almost everyone in the packed room rises to their feet and cheers; I sit there silently, still shaking from the strain of asking the question. I wish so much that I could join in the applause, and share the community feeling that usually makes me so happy.

Yet, at the same time, I also recognize that this scene exemplifies the problem which I had tried to raise, whether democracy could be won through undemocratic means. I'm angry at the other organizers for taking the easy way out, but mostly at Cesar because he knows better and is letting this happen, even orchestrating it. He taught me what organizing is about: empowerment. And yet here he is, courting a leader who didn't want to empower anybody, and, worse, encouraging his own followers to surrender to him the power to decide what is true and what is false.

These two memories, particularly the last one, have haunted me as an activist, and as a teacher of activism. My experience with the United Farm Workers revealed the danger as well as the promise of participatory politics; Cesar exemplified both the empowering and disempowering leader and teacher. At his best, Cesar *was* a great leader, but not because people followed him blindly. To me, he led by encouraging all of us to discover our own capacities for leadership.

My original decision to join the UFW was impulsive. In August 1974, frustrated at the gap between studying and practicing democracy, I began a year's leave of absence from the graduate program in political science at the University of California at Berkeley. While visiting friends in New York City, a day or so before stepping on a plane for Europe, I happened to see an ad in the *Village Voice*. The small box said something like, "In six months, Cesar Chavez will teach you to organize." Six months of community organizing would still leave six months for hitchhiking across Europe, and such a modest investment in direct action seemed like a good way to ease both my guilt about my political passivity and my doubts about leaving graduate school.

Although my friends and I had boycotted grapes, iceberg lettuce, and Gallo wines, along with my friends I actually knew very little about the farmworkers' lengthy struggle to win union representation. I also had only the vaguest notion of what an organizer actually did. I suppose that I saw myself as "helping" farmworkers, giving them the benefit of my time and knowledge as a middle-class college graduate.

But I quickly discovered that volunteering with the UFW was not about charity, but about justice, not about "doing good," but sharing the struggle. Years later, Nadinne Cruz, a wonderful community activist and teacher, taught me an Aboriginal expression that captures the mutual relationship between the organizer and the people: "If you've come to help me, no thank you. But if your liberation is bound up with mine, then come, let us work together."[4]

Participatory politics in the United Farm Workers meant, simply, that farmworkers and volunteer organizers worked together to develop our strategies and put them into action. On a personal level, participation enabled me to be fully myself, with others, in a way that I had never experienced before. For the first time, I understood what the political theorist Hannah Arendt meant by "the joy in action," even though some of the action was distinctly joyless.[5]

It was exhilarating as well as bone chilling to hold up our signs to the early morning traffic on the George Washington Bridge. Somehow, I managed to wave to the cars which honked sympathetically, while hanging onto the sign that the icy wind tried to rip from my grasp. I was less enthusiastic about our pre-dawn trips to picket the Hunt's Point Market, where Teamster truckdrivers glared and cursed our pititful attempts to persuade them not to unload crates of "scab" grapes and lettuce. Once, an African American owner of a liquor store pulled a gun on me when I asked him to support the Gallo wine boycott. "How can he do this?" I asked myself, as I walked backwards, carefully and I hoped calmly, unable to take my eyes off what seemed to be at least a foot-wide barrel. "Most of the farmworkers have been discriminated against, just like him." Then with distance came reflection: "What am I doing here? A white girl trying to tell blacks what to do?"

Yet, after six months, I sold back my ticket. I stayed with the UFW for the next four years, the last three as an organizer in the fields of California. It was such an exciting period: organizing campaigns in which farmworkers could vote, for the first time in American history, for a union to represent them, then figuring out with them how to negotiate and to administer the first collective bargaining agreements. I learned Spanish on the run, from the farmworkers whom I organized; I never mastered the grammar, but I was very strong on fruits and vegetables. I felt as if I was helping to make history, part of building a movement that aimed not only to improve the lives of farmworkers, but to make the country and the world more just and more democratic.

However, in 1976, I left the United Farm Workers Union over its failure to practice internally the democracy it preached. I spent the next ten years in the labor movement, as a telephone operator and rank-and-file steward with the Communications Workers of America (CWA), and as a field representative with Service Employees International Union (SEIU) Locals 535 and 715 in California's Silicon

Valley. Today, as a beginning professor, I am less naive, but still committed to teaching about and working for democracy.

How can I, as an activist, contribute to the building of a democratic movement, while helping the community organizations with which I work remain democratic? How can I, as a teacher, help my students to see the difficulties as well as the joys of participatory politics without adding to their cynicism about the possibility of political change? On good days, I think that I've gotten close to an answer. I am the professor of Democratic Theory and Practice in the Department of Political Science at Swarthmore College, which is, to my knowledge, the only such position in the country. I also direct the Democracy Project, which "encourages students to deepen their understanding of and commitment to democratic participation in a multicultural nation, through community action." Translated from the language of college catalogs, this means that students learn about participatory politics through participating, as interns with local community service and advocacy organizations.

On bad days, I feel like a fake. I imagine colleagues, students, and even activists accusing me of hypocrisy, or worse. A professor criticizes my pretensions: "What are you saying? Surely, you don't mean to suggest that all professors should be activists and write books about action? Or, maybe you believe that they should stop publishing altogether?" "No!" I try to sound more confident than I feel. "I mean, if I believed that, I wouldn't be writing this book." "Then, is all this talk about action anything more than grandstanding? And what about the value of objectivity? Don't you think that a teacher should allow her students to make up their own minds?" As I rack my brains to come up with a convincing retort, the interrogator pushes ahead, relentlessly. "You couldn't possibly claim that a biased scholar can discover the truth? And isn't knowledge necessary for political action? You yourself have just told us a story about the disastrous consequences of the farmworkers' misunderstanding of leadership. Of course, such anecdotal evidence is of limited usefulness...."

I have barely begun to respond when an activist interrupts: "Come on, Meta. You're just pretending to combine teaching, scholarship, and activism. What a hypocrite! Are you really accomplishing anything, besides beefing up enrollment in your classes—at least until the next fad comes along? Get real. You're just trying to ease your guilt about leaving the streets for the comfortable academy."

A student chimes in, with another telling accusation: "It's soooooo boring. I'm tired of hearing about the sixties from nostalgic activists trying to make me feel guilty. Face it. It's got nothing to do with us." I want to point out that I'm a seventies and not a sixties activist, but then I'm reminded of the time when my daughter Jackie came home from elementary school on Halloween, overflowing with excitement about the great costumes her classmates wore: "...and Sarah was...." A pause as she tries to remember the name of her friend's choice. Then a triumphant smile: "A hippie!" The puzzled look returns to her face. "Do you know what that is, Mommy?" To my own daughter, the sixties were a prehistoric era, just after the dinosaurs maybe.

Frankly, I am not at all sure that writing a book about the national memory of the sixties will help to reclaim democracy in the nineties. And trying to combine activism, teaching, and scholarship often seems both inadequate and impossible. But what is the alternative? To acquiesce in the widening gap between Americans with political, economic, and social resources and power, and those who are poor, labelled by the color of their skin, their gender, the country of their ancestors, or other badges of difference, continually reminded that they are or should be powerless? Or, to engage in conventional politics by signing a petition, voting, or working for the candidate whose views seem to be least distant from mine?

But, my organizing experience has taught me that only a democratic movement can bring about significant political change. And I see the hopeful beginnings of such a movement in local communities where people have begun, despite many obstacles, to reclaim control over their neighborhoods and workplaces.[6] Access to the hidden heritage of the sixties could help these scattered experiments in participatory politics come together in a democratic movement for democracy.

So, I am encouraged when students, excited about their own activist experiences, ask me to tell them about my activism, what I did and what I do. Jackie, too, wants to hear the story of the battered red flag which I have from a farmworkers strike years ago. I can pass along my personal memories to my daughter and to my students, but what has happened to our collective memory of participatory politics during the sixties and throughout American history? How do we tell the democratic story of the sixties, and could it be told in a way that helps to reclaim democracy?

ONE

REMEMBERING DEMOCRACY

IN 1993, the bookstore at Swarthmore College, where I teach political science, created a display commemorating the thirtieth anniversary of student involvement in the civil rights movement here at the college. The display featured huge blowups of pages from the school newspaper the *Phoenix*, and other local newspapers containing articles about the campaign against discrimination in the schools in the nearby city of Chester. On November 16, 1963, for instance, the *Phoenix* reports that the Chester school board has agreed to the major demands of the protestors, following two weeks of demonstrations in which 240 people were arrested, including fifty-seven Swarthmore students. Looking back almost thirty years later, these pages seem quaint; the front-page articles on the local civil rights movement nestle up to more conventional pieces on the college's plan to build a new library, and on a botany lecture which is part of "the recent movement to make Swarthmore students more aware of 'the trees and flowers.'"[1] The following week, on November 23, 1963, the *Phoenix* juxtaposes an editorial denouncing the administration's threat to discipline student protestors, with an account of a survey to be distributed to students in the dining hall to determine their food preferences.[2]

Most of the people in the towns around the college were dismayed by the students' activism, as blowups from local newspapers make clear. An article from the *Philadelphia Daily News* reports that the former chair of the Chester Human Relations Commission has "blasted" the Swarthmore students for their participation in the "riotous civil rights demonstrations that plagued Chester last week."[3] In the *Chester Pennsylvania Times*, a debate rages over whether the students should get involved in the civil rights movement. Most of the letter writers say no, emphatically; as a Chester resident put it, "Instead of getting an education, which some people can't even afford, they are inciting riots and acting like a bunch of un-American radicals." However, at least one other writer expresses her

> heartfelt thanks and deep appreciation...to those brave and dedicated students who did participate in recent demonstrations. While some might condemn them now, it is certain that the future will honor them.[4]

She was wrong. The many anonymous participants in the sixties movements have been largely forgotten. On the rare occasions when the future does take note, it is to condemn not to honor them.

A small box on the front page of the November 23, 1963, edition of the *Phoenix* suggests what *is* remembered from the sixties. Tucked in among the articles on the demonstrations and on college events is a "Late Notice: The Haverford soccer and football games have been cancelled because of the death of President Kennedy. They will probably be played at a later date."[5] History does not record whether Swarthmore and Haverford replayed their matches, but no one today doubts the significance of the Kennedy assassination in our national memory of the sixties. Today, the students who read the *Phoenix* thirty years ago may have only a vague recollection of the arrests of their classmates, but, like me, they probably remember exactly where they were when they heard that the President had been shot. What do their children "remember"?

Recently, a historian and I team-taught a course on the sixties. Enrollment was large, although we weren't sure why. Because students were drawn to the subject matter? To the professors? To the movies and the music? Because they needed a political science or history course? A course that was offered at 11:20 on Tuesdays and Thursdays? Because they wanted to understand their parents (students actually told us this)? Or simply because it sounded easy? Although some students seemed to be disappointed that we didn't take what they thought of as a sixties approach to the assignments (i.e., we graded them), they seemed to enjoy the course (at least, few dropped it). But, what did they learn?

To my surprise, nearly all of the American students came to the course with strong opinions on the sixties, despite knowing very little of the actual history. This is not really their fault: except for the few who had already studied some American history in college, most students had taken standard high school courses which barely got through World War II. In fact, the strength of their views appeared to be inversely related to their knowledge.

For instance, many students argued that John F. Kennedy was a much better President than the course texts made him out to be, and that he would surely have ended the Vietnam War if only he had not been assassinated. This opinion puzzled me, until I realized that most of them had learned about the sixties from movies. Their image of the martyred saint, overly simplified at best, came from Oliver Stone's *JFK*.

As an activist, I was especially disappointed to find that many students began the course deeply hostile to the sixties movements, even though they knew little or nothing about participatory democracy. The New Leftists were just kids who wanted to have fun (my students had heard about Woodstock or seen it on video), while the civil rights movement meant only the assassination of Martin Luther King, busing, and Black Power. Few recognized the names Student Nonviolent Coordinating Committee (SNCC), and no one seemed to know that the slogan "Black Power" originated in SNCC's efforts to build independent, militant-but-nonviolent organizations in the rural South.

My lecture on the original Black Panther Party, which was founded in Lowndes County, Alabama, as part of the struggle for voting rights, could not compete with the powerful images they'd seen, on television or in photographs of the Oakland Black Panthers brandishing rifles. To most of our white students, Black Power was simply a synonym for violence. In the most heated discussion of the term, several students, mostly white, criticized the use of violence, and several others, mostly African American, defended it, while the rest of the group remained silent, hoping that the tension or the class would be over soon. Yet, the study of the sixties offered those students who were courageous enough to take advantage of it, the opportunity to talk openly about race, a subject that is rarely discussed in mixed groups.

Still, only the few student activists seemed to want to learn more about the nonviolent experiments in participatory democracy, which brought together people of different races and backgrounds to fight for justice. At times, I felt as if we were offering the students in the class a kind of historical smorgasbord from which they could pick only those events that confirmed their cynicism about politics, and reject the rest.

However, only one semester after our course, an outbreak of racist and homophobic graffiti on campus sparked students into action. A sit-in at the administration building was followed by rallies and marches against hate speech. I was impressed by the number and diversity of students practicing the participatory politics of the sixties, even if most of them would have denied the analogy.

The stereotype of the apathetic "Generation X," so-called by everyone except its own members, ignores the reappearance of participatory politics on campus such as the nationwide demonstrations that followed the passage of California's anti-immigrant Proposition 187, in 1994. Swarthmore College students formed the multiracial Coalition Against Xenophobia (CAX), which led hundreds of Philadelphia-area students, and a few community members and faculty, on an exuberant march around the Liberty Bell on a very cold and rainy December afternoon. Although these protests received a few seconds of television coverage and a newspaper article here and there, brief glimpses of young activists engaged in nonviolent protest cannot compete with the image of participatory politics that dominates nineties political culture: the self-indulgent or gunwielding sixties "rebels."

If the Swarthmore college bookstore had been designed to reflect the national memory of the sixties, there would have been far less attention paid to the political actions of ordinary people. Instead, the bookstore might have reproduced large blowups of the Kennedy and King assassinations, along with photographs of angry demonstrators running through the streets and, of course, the Black Panthers. Or, the display could have featured the postgraduate career of a Swarthmore student whose name appears in the list of those arrested, Cathy Wilkerson.

In 1963, Cathy Wilkerson was one of "the Swarthmore girls who are making all the trouble," according to the exasperated warden of the jail where the demonstrators "stomped, yelled, shouted, and sang all night."[6] In 1970, Cathy Wikerson narrowly escaped dying in the accidental explosion of a bomb which destroyed her father's plush New York City townhouse. At the time, Wilkerson was one of the Weathermen, former members of the Students for a Democratic Society, who had left SDS in order to make the "revolution" through terrorism. Three of Wilkerson's young comrades died in the blast, including Terry Robbins, whose body was so completely mutilated that he could not even be identified for many months. Wilkerson herself disappeared into "the underground"; after years on the run, she finally turned herself in.[7]

To many people, the townhouse explosion came to symbolize the self-destructiveness of the decade. So, the college bookstore might have displayed a photo of the rubble next to the article on the student arrests. From singing songs to making bombs, Cathy Wilkerson's life represents the prevailing interpretation of the sixties as a chamber of horrors which we might want to remember as a cautionary tale, but surely not revive.

The Sixties Are Dead?

In a recent column entitled "Slamming the Doors," the conservative columnist George Will denounced one of the recent crop of sixties movies:

> The problem is juvenophilia. It is the foolishness of listening for wisdom from the mouths of babes and hoping that youthful

> vigor (that favorite word along the New Frontier when the
> Sixties were aborning) will liberate by smashing old
> structures.... The central myth of the Sixties was that the
> wretched excess was really a serious quest for new values.[8]

Will concludes, with relief, that the period is over:
"The Sixties are dead. Not a moment too soon." Yet, he
admits that "there will always be a few who seek
salvation from cathartic rock music, orgasmic politics
and pornography masquerading as social profundity."[9]
If that is so, then maybe the sixties are not safely dead.
What else explains the urgency of devoting a two-page
column to "slamming the doors"?

George Will demonstrates, in spite of himself, the
truth of William Faulkner's famous pronouncement:
"The past isn't dead. It isn't even past." The sixties live
on—as metaphor, positive and negative, accurate and
inaccurate. In American politics, the sixties stand in for
the idea of a more participatory democracy: our images
of the civil rights movement and the New Left shape
and reflect our attitudes toward greater participation
in politics today. In this respect, our memories of the
sixties serve a function analogous to that of an earlier
generation's memories of the popular movements of
the thirties. The images of people marching in the
streets could have recalled to them either the inspiring
struggle of poor people to form labor unions and to
claim their full rights as human beings or the terrifying
specter of ignorant masses manipulated by fascist

leaders. The national memory of the sixties is also contested, but dominated by frightening visions of a generation run amok.

But, then, what explains the astonishing resurgence of interest in the sixties? In national politics, recent Presidents have sought to define themselves in reference to the decade. During the 1992 Presidential election campaign, Bill Clinton tried to drape himself in the mantle of President John F. Kennedy, while his predecessor, George Bush, frequently attacked his opponents as "remnants of the 1960s, the New Left, campus radicals grown old, the peace marchers and the nuclear-freeze activists."[10] During the 1991 Gulf War, both proponents and critics of the war appealed to the analogy of the sixties, particularly the "Vietnam syndrome."[11] In many other public controversies, from the status of women to the state of the labor movement, activists and observers offer the sixties as evidence.[12] In 1992, conservatives blamed the Los Angeles riots on the liberal policies of the sixties.[13] On campus, the acrimonious debates over "political correctness" often become battles about the legacy of the sixties.[14]

The reappearance of the sixties in political discourse has been accompanied by a renaissance in popular culture, including movies, television, music, fiction, and even fashion, as my daughter's devotion to tie-dye has taught me. During the summer of 1994, hundreds of thousands of people headed toward upstate New York to relive or reenact the original Woodstock festival. Other examples include the movies *Forrest Gump, The Doors, Malcolm X, Mississippi Burning,* and *JFK*; the television shows, "Eyes on the Prize: America's Civil Rights Years," and "The Wonder Years"; the novels *Vineland* and *Making Peace*; and the renewed popularity of sixties clothing, and rock and roll.[15]

In addition to numerous references to the sixties in print and television journalism, a number of popular and scholarly books on the decade have been published during the last few years, along with many articles and reviews. Among the most significant books are Taylor Branch, *Parting the Waters: America in the King Years 1954–63*; Elaine Brown, *A Taste of Power: A Black Woman's Story*; Peter Collier and David Horowitz, *Destructive Generation: Second Thoughts About the Sixties*; Todd Gitlin, *The Sixties: Years of Hope, Days of Rage*; and James Miller, *"Democracy Is in the Streets": From Port Huron to the Siege of Chicago*.[16]

But, perhaps the current groundswell of attention to the sixties is misleading, merely a temporary phenomenon. The baby boomers are getting older, so naturally they're interested in the anniversaries of the major events of their youth, such as the March on Washington and the Kennedy assassination in 1963, and the Apollo moon landing and the Woodstock festival in 1969. They're also the main audience for television and print coverage of the recent deaths of sixties heroes and villains including Richard Nixon, Jacqueline Kennedy Onassis, and Abbie Hoffman. But many of their children seem to be uninterested, bored, or resentful.

For instance, Lorraine Ali, a young pop music critic, compared her parents' reactions to the murder of sixties icon, John Lennon, to her own response to the suicide of nineties rock star, Kurt Cobain:

> The 60s is an era that my peers and I are constantly reminded we missed. A great time when teens were filled with good vibes and didn't blow each other away over a pair of Adidases. They were blessed with naivete and denial—they believed all things could be good if you tried hard enough.
>
> Kurt Cobain was one among a league of kids raised by sixties parents who shuffled their children from relative to relative in a quest for personal freedom.... They suffered the fallout of free love, and as adults, they sell millions of records to peers who can relate to their rootless anger and dysfunction.[17]

While Cobain certainly did not invent alienation, resentment, and anger toward the older generation, the boomers might feel that they are being attacked from both sides. Surprisingly, Lorraine Ali and George Will agree in blaming the sixties, although Will would probably see Kurt Cobain as the latest youth to be seduced by cathartic rock music, orgasmic politics, and pornography. The political conservative and the hip rock critic both want to slam the door on the sixties.

Perhaps, once all the sixties celebrities are buried, the next generation will have taken over and there will be no more talk about reviving the sixties, in politics or anywhere else. Each state funeral seems to produce the announcement, "the end of an era," almost like a ritual incantation. But it must not be a very effective one, since the era seems to keep rising out of the grave, to haunt us until the next death and attempted burial.

In February 1994, nearly two decades after the Vietnam War ended, President Bill Clinton announced that the United States would finally lift its economic embargo against its former enemy. "The nation is one," Clinton proclaimed; our country, which had been so divided over the war, was reunited at last. The *New York Times* proclaimed: "A Passion Spent...Clinton relegates the Vietnam War to the national memory."[18]

But what is the national memory? The *Times* implies that it is something like a vault where provocative images, and the dangerous emotions to which they give rise, are permanently sequestered. Hatred, fear, distrust, doubt—all locked away behind reinforced steel walls. This vision of the national memory allows us to forget what is too painful to remember.

But what exactly has been relegated to the national memory? What is the passion that has finally been spent and locked away? Here is an image that comes to my mind:

A crowded sidewalk in front of City Hall, with lots of

traffic whizzing by. It's a hot, sticky summer day in New York City, the air is heavy with the smells of exhaust, sweat, hot dogs, occasional overpowering whiffs of perfume from passersby. It's noisy, too; horns honk above the sounds of machinery, foreign accents, New Yawk tawk, shouts. On the sidewalk, angry supporters of the Vietnam War confront a straggly band of antiwar protestors. Heavily muscled construction workers, faces contorted with rage beneath dented hard hats, scream "Love it or leave it!" Frightened, jeans-clad young women and men wave handwritten signs, chanting "Hey, hey, LBJ, how many kids did you kill today?" and "Hell no, we won't go!" One skinny, long-haired demonstrator gets into a shouting match with a beefy hard hat, each hurling "fuck you's" at the other. All of a sudden, someone throws a rock, and the crowd of construction workers surges into the line of protestors. The young people try to fend off blows or to get away, a woman falls to the ground. Cardboard signs are trampled, a pair of granny glasses is broken, the woman moans in pain. The police look away, faint smirks on their faces.

My mental image disturbs me, especially the clichés and stereotypes. All supporters of the war weren't construction workers (and all construction workers aren't beefy), while some protestors were violent themselves, or simply self-interested, paying little attention to the war until the draft was extended to college students like themselves. Perhaps someone else around my age remembers the antiwar protestors as angry and threatening. Maybe, she sees them with dirty, long hair flying, as they curse, spit upon, and throw rocks at clean-cut young draftees about to enter an induction center. To her, the soldiers and the supporters of the war were true patriots, to the point of risking their lives, or their sons' lives, for democracy and freedom.

Oddly, my mental image doesn't reflect accurately my personal experience as an antiwar demonstrator during the early seventies. Although I do remember being charged by the police and the national guard, I don't think that I ever saw any hard hats, except on television. Yet, I imagine myself as one of the protestors under attack by hard hats, even if I was never in exactly that situation. In fact, my memory picture seems really to be a kind of collage of my own experiences, media scenes, and my studies.

Does my more conservative counterpart have a similar mix of private and public images, although with a different sense of personal identification? What about people of different races, ethnicities, classes, genders, sexual preferences, religions? Do people who share one or more of these "identities" necessarily share the same memories? Does another progressive activist like me remember the sixties in the same way that I do?

What kind of memories do people who are younger than either of us have? Although they do not remember personally supporting or opposing the war, my students' mental images are not pure reflections of the media or history books, either. Their memories are also filtered through personal experience, such as listening to a relative's stories or watching the latest war movie. What do you remember?

Somehow, these personal memories, unique mixtures of direct and indirect experience, media, history, popular culture, and individual circumstances, add up to the national memory, the story we tell ourselves about our collective past. Unfortunately for Presidents, the image of a storage vault fails to capture how contested, volatile, and passionate the national memory really is.

It is time to look critically at the resurgence of interest in the sixties, and to bring to light the significant role played by our memories of the sixties in the politics and culture of the nineties. Most of the recent books on the sixties have been histories, of specific events or of the decade as a whole. In political science, scholars have focused on national politics, and on leaders who achieved national stature, paying much less attention to the grassroots movements and the people who participated in them. Hundreds of books have been written about the John F. Kennedy assassination, for instance, but there have been only two significant histories of the most participatory organization of the sixties: the Student Nonviolent Coordinating Committee (SNCC).[19] Although scholars have begun to study the memory of specific national events, such as the JFK assassination and Watergate, no one has addressed the way in which the myth of the sixties has been used to discourage popular participation in politics.[20]

As an activist committed to a truly democratic America, I am most concerned about the sixties as a political metaphor, specifically, a metaphor for participatory politics. Therefore, this book does *not* focus on sixties culture (e.g. "sex, drugs, and rock and roll," Elvis, Jimi, Janis, the Beatles, the Stones, surfboards, beehives, split-levels, pillbox hats, marijuana, LSD, strobe lights, lava lamps, bellbottoms, headbands, beads, Haight-Ashbury, Andy Warhol, *The Graduate, Easy Rider, The Man from U.N.C.L.E*), nor all of sixties politics (e.g., civil rights legislation, the Vietnam War, the War on Poverty, the military-industrial complex), except insofar as these topics shed light on the way in which memories of the sixties affect the prospects for participatory politics in the nineties.

Although this book addresses American politics, the memory of the sixties is an international phenomenon, just as the sixties movements were. For instance, toward the end of 1989, a *New York Times* headline proclaimed that the "Spirit of 1968 Is Still Alive." A science writer added that "The same spirit is here today."[21] The speakers were Czechoslovakians, participants in the popular movement that swept the Communists from power in one of the revolutions of 1989. The memory of "Prague Spring," repressed under Communism, was recovered during the first heady moments of the Velvet Revolution. But scarcely two years later, the "Spirit of 1968" had gone out of fashion again. A journalist reported that "the so-called generation of '68 has come under attack as democracy and market economies have pulled younger Czechs and Slavs to the right."[22] Perhaps, as countries around the world embrace American-style politics and economics, their views on the sixties come to resemble our own.

For most Americans, "politics" means the government. In this book, the term "politics," encompasses a wide range of activities having to do with the life we share as members of a community. "Participatory politics" refers to the most direct possible participation of each of us in the political decision-making process. Politics is the answer to the question, "What shall we do?"; participatory politics occurs when *we* answer it together. How we do this is by no means simple, but more specific definitions of what counts as politics and participation ought to be made by the people themselves. By deciding what to do we also decide who we are, over and over again.[23]

Like other metaphors, "the sixties" is an image that

stands in for something else, in a way that both enables and hinders understanding and communication. Political metaphors direct our gaze toward certain facets of complex, emotionally charged concepts or issues, by lifting our eyes from other ones. In the United States, the sixties have been most frequently used to highlight the negative experience of participatory politics, while obscuring the positive.

The dominant memory of the sixties both reflects and shapes the national turn away from popular participation during recent decades. Less than half of the adult population votes in Presidential elections, probably the least demanding of political activities. More active forms of participation, such as working for a candidate or just putting up a lawn sign, have also declined. When I compare my students to myself and my friends in college (1968-72), I see a lot of the same cynicism, but a different attitude toward doing something about it. Where many of us felt that we could and ought to try to make a difference, most young people now, like their parents, view politics as a dirty activity that only makes things worse. Except for commencement exercises, when the graduates are enjoined to save the world, the message that students receive from society is: don't get involved in politics, except for self-defense. It's almost impossible to imagine a nineties President repeating John Kennedy's famous words: "Ask not what your country can do for you, but what you can do for your country."

The dramatic rejection of the Democratic Party in the 1994 elections reveals not the determination of people to take back their country, but the depth of their frustration and anger. The Republican Party, which in 1994 took control of Congress for the first time in forty years, is even less likely than its predecessor to open the political system to those who have been excluded. In fact, the new politics openly pits white men, the rich, and the upper middle class against people of color, women, and the poor. During the 1990s, the most effective practitioners of a kind of participatory politics have been the Christian fundamentalists, who aim to restore hierarchy in government and society. The progressives who favor a more participatory democracy are nearly invisible on the national political scene, while the majority of Americans have given up on the one alleged power they still possess: the vote.

Yet, many people sense that there is a gap between the American ideal and experience of democracy. As a sandwich shop operator in Chicago put it:

> To me, neither side does anything for you, so it doesn't matter how you vote. We're worried about where the country's going, but we can't change anything, not anything. It's scary. It's not supposed to be this way.[24]

The speaker feels powerless and hopeless, but also cheated; she senses that a citizen of the oldest democracy in the world should not feel as she does.

American political science has generally taken the position that it is supposed to be this way, that democracy works best when most people accept a passive role in politics. In the conclusion to their influential study of voting, frequently assigned in introductory political science courses, Bernard R. Berelson, Paul F. Lazarsfeld, and William N. McPhee ask:

> How could a mass democracy work if all the people were deeply involved in politics? Lack of interest by some people is not without its benefits, too. True, the highly interested voters vote more, and know more about the campaign, and read and listen more, and participate more; however, they are also less open to persuasion and less likely to change. Exteme interest goes with extreme partisanship and might culminate in rigid fanaticism that could destroy democratic processes if generalized throughout the community.... Some people are and should be highly interested in politics, but not everyone is or needs to be. Only the doctrinaire would deprecate the moderate indifference that facilitates compromise.[25]

The classic theoretical argument against political participation was made by Joseph Schumpeter. Because "the electoral mass is incapable of action other than a stampede," it is better for all concerned to accept that "democracy is the rule of the politician."[26]

However, a few political scientists and theorists have questioned whether a democratic system premised upon the lack of participation of the majority is, in fact, a democracy.[27] Yet, these sophisticated writings are almost unreadable to most of the people whom they want to participate. Neither political science nor political theory has addressed the way in which our memories of the most recent participatory era in American history limit democratic possibilities in the present and the future. As the United States again approaches a political crisis over poverty and racial inequality, the lessons of the sixties become even more relevant. What if the sandwich shop operator, and all Americans, knew the full story of the sixties movements for democracy?

"What Our Past is Going to Be"

Although the national memory of the sixties distorts and threatens to erase much of the political history of the decade, it remains contested. The old East European jest, "We don't know yet what our past is going to be," applies to Americans, too.[28] We still do not know what our memory of the sixties is going to be, because political memory is part of what Richard Slotkin, in his pathbreaking history of American culture, has described as "a continuous dialectic between cultural discourse, material conditions, social and political actions."[29] Our memories of the sixties help to shape the culture, economy, society, and politics of the nineties, which help to shape our memories of the sixties, which help to shape the culture, economy, society, and politics of the nineties, and so on.

Scholars in the relatively new field of the history of

memory have shown that at certain historical moments, the national memory of an earlier period can become a focal point for contemporary struggles over divisive issues. As Krzystof Pomian explains, "when the time is right, an era of the past may serve as a screen on which new generations can project their contradictions, controversies, and conflicts in objectified form."[30] An example is France's Vichy period; the historian Henry Rousso has argued that an official memory of collaboration with the Nazis competes with countermemories, in a complex, multilevel, and dynamic contest over the direction of French politics today.[31] Similarly, what is at stake in the American struggle over who owns the sixties is ownership of the nineties.

Pierre Nora, the foremost historian of memory, calls these problematic eras "sites of memory (*lieux de memoire*)." He contrasts these to "environments of memory (*milieux de memoire*)," which, like the vibrant nineteenth-century American communities described by Alexis Tocqueville, link people to their ancestors, to their descendants and to their contemporaries.[32] Nowadays, environments of memory are but a memory themselves, superseded but not replaced by sites of memory. Yet, people still long to recapture the lost connection to the past; as Nora points out, "We speak so much of memory because there is so little of it left."[33]

In a similar vein, Hannah Arendt, the great twentieth-century political theorist, observed that "the thread of tradition is broken and we must discover our past for ourselves."[34] But how do we do that? Should we even try? Karl Marx, like many other activists and theorists, believed that political movements should look not backward but forward, drawing their "poetry [not] from the past, but only from the future."[35] To Arendt, our ability to act politically, to begin something new, depends on knowing where we have come from and where we are.[36] During the sixties, she tried to pass on the tale of the lost tradition of participatory politics, with the hope of supporting and educating the young participants in the latest democratic moment.

The rest of this book aims to tell the story of the relationship of the sixties to the nineties, by comparing our memories to the history of participatory politics in the civil rights movement and the New Left. Instead of drawing inspiration and valuable lessons, positive and negative, from the country's most recent experience of participation on a large scale, we have nearly forgotten that ordinary people took democratic action to bring about more democracy, and could do so again.

The point is not to discover the past in order simply to reenact it. There is a lot that we would not want to repeat, even if we could. Instead, I hope to help today's students and activists recognize how misunderstanding the past constrains the choices we make in the present for the future, which after all will be *their* future.

But how do we compare memories to the history of the sixties? Do we even know what is "memory" and what is "history"? Scholars have shown that, on the one hand, there is no "pure," or memory-free, history, and on the other, that memory contains fact as well as distortion.[37] However, to say that it is impossible to draw the line, once and for all, in every case, does not mean that there is no difference between memory and history, or that there is nothing to be gained by looking at what our memories of the sixties include and exclude. Although the sixties are contested, there are general themes which make it possible to discuss and perhaps reach agreement on the meaning of the era in contemporary politics. For the purposes of this study, it may be enough to be self-conscious about the interrelationship between memory and history and to be aware that any definition of the national memory is necessarily tentative and contestable.

How do we measure the national memory? Is collective memory anything more than the sum of individual memories? Perhaps we should just conduct a poll, and the final result will be the national memory— for the moment at least. And the reader would be free to accept or reject the aggregate memory, depending on how close it comes to her own personal or acquired "memory." Such an approach would, however, distort the complex montage that is the national memory into something that could be measured quantitatively. In reality, the national memory of the sixties reveals itself through references to the decade in political and popular culture.[38]

Although this book is grounded in the fields of political theory, the history of memory, and American studies, its persuasiveness rests ultimately upon a participatory approach to knowledge. I invite you to open yourself to a range of other people's memories and to consider your own self—critically. I have expressed openly my own commitment to participatory politics, because neither the writer nor the reader comes to this material neutrally. Before I write or you read a page, we have memories of the sixties, and we have views on the possibility or desirability of greater participation in politics—even if our view is simply that it's boring. In a way, this is both an author's dream and nightmare, that her readers already know and have opinions about her subject.

Yet, I also hope that reading this book is more than just a consumer activity, in which readers "shop" for the memories and histories that are closest to their own, that make them feel good, or that are preferable in other ways. In any event, I cannot make you read this book in a certain way, any more than I can make you read it at all. Even if I could, I would not. Reclaiming democracy, and reading books about it, are ultimately up to the people, including you.

TWO

"THE TRUE DEMOCRACY"

AT the 1964 Democratic National Party Convention, Fannie Lou Hamer, a middle-aged black sharecropper, was a leader of the Mississippi Freedom Democratic Party (MFDP) delegation. Because they had been chosen in an election open to all adults, black and white, Hamer and the other MFDP delegates claimed that they should be seated in place of the regular, all-white state delegation. When a reporter asked Hamer if she was seeking total equality between the races she told him, "What would I look like fighting for equality with the white man? I don't want to go down that low. I want the true democracy that'll raise me and that white man up...raise America up."[1] Hamer's words, "the true democracy," capture the history of the sixties that has been largely forgotten: the attempt to practice a participatory kind of democracy that would raise not just blacks, but all of America, up.

During the era of the civil rights movement and the New Left, groups of activists fought not only for the rights of all Americans to participate in politics, but also for a redefinition of the meaning of political participation. The Student Nonviolent Coordinating Committee (SNCC), which organized the MFDP, and the Students for a Democratic Society (SDS) conducted the two most significant experiments in participatory democracy. Both groups attempted, and briefly succeeded in practicing a politics based on the SNCC slogan, "We are all leaders."[2]

The "Redemptive Community"

SNCC was founded in 1960 by Southern black college students who had begun "sitting-in" at segregated lunch counters earlier that year. Television pictures and newspaper photographs of angry whites pouring catsup and hot coffee on the peaceful, neatly dressed young people had shocked the country, and inspired other students to sit-in, too. In April, the leaders came together to found a new kind of organization, a "redemptive community."[3] They committed themselves to living their vision of a democratic, interracial community within SNCC, as the best way of redeeming the community around them. James Forman, an SNCC chairman, described the organization, in phrases that were widely repeated, as "a band of brothers, standing in a circle of love."[4] To its members, the redemptive community was "everything: home and family, food and work, love and a reason to live."[5]

Although not a community organization itself (only full-time organizers could belong), SNCC aimed to build grassroots movements in Southern rural towns, where segregation and poverty were at their worst. The organizers—blacks and whites, men and women, middle class and poor, students and sharecroppers— worked and lived together on subsistence stipends, under constant threat of harassment and violence. SNCC grew rapidly, and soon became notable within the civil rights movement for its internal democracy, its militancy, and the way in which its organizers entered into the life of the people, helping them to become, in essence, their own organizers.

SNCC tried to open people's eyes to the gap between

the ideal and the reality of American democracy. A leaflet distributed in Mississippi to protest the Vietnam War asked why black soldiers should defend democracy abroad when they were denied it at home:

> We can write and ask our sons if they know what they are fighting for. If he answers Freedom, tell him that's what we are fighting for here in Mississippi. And if he says democracy, tell him the truth—we don't know anything about Communism, Socialism, and all that, but we do know that Negroes have caught hell here under this *American Democracy*.[6] (italics in original)

Instead, SNCC invited blacks to fight non-violently, here in the United States, for the "true" democracy. The rallying cry, "we are all leaders," meant more than that each person has the capacity for leadership. A genuine democracy would not have leaders in the usual sense, because each person would participate equally in doing what leaders do now: making and carrying out political decisions. There would be no hierarchy, no separation between the leaders and the led. Unlike other major civil rights organizations, which emphasized litigation and legislation, SNCC focused, in the words of Reverend James Lawson, on "developing our greatest resource, a people no longer the victims of racial evil who can act in a disciplined manner to implement the Constitution."[7]

Self-transformation was the first step in developing a people who can act politically. Once transformed, individuals would transform their communities through nonviolent protest. Bernice Johnson Reagon, now the leader of the influential black acapella singing group Sweet Honey in the Rock, joined SNCC as a student at historically black Albany State College in Georgia. She remembers:

> The voice I have now I got the first time I sang in a movement meeting, after I got out of jail. I did the song, "Over My Head I See Freedom in the Air," but I had never heard that voice before. I had never been that me before. And once I became that me, I have never let that me go.... [A] transformation took place inside of the people. The singing was just the echo of that.[8]

This sensation of a new "me" was shared by many participants in the movement. Hartman Turnbow, a farmer whose house was firebombed after he tried to register to vote, says: "I don't know where all that braveness came from. I just found myself, I just found myself with it."[9] Similarly, SNCC organizer Diane Nash recalls that "the movement had a way of reaching inside you and bringing out things that even you didn't know were there."[10]

In SNCC's view, only a truly democratic "movement," not a hierarchical organization, could promote this kind of self-transformation. Ella Baker, the civil rights veteran who organized the conference at which SNCC was founded, expressed what was distinctive about the new group: "Instead of 'the leader,' a person who was supposed to be a magic man, you would develop individuals who were bound together by a concept that provided an opportunity for them to grow into being responsible."[11]

Bob Moses, the self-effacing organizer who came to symbolize SNCC's unusual approach to leadership, explained the philosophy behind it:

> Leadership is there in the people. You don't have to worry about that. You don't have to worry about where your leaders are, how are we going to get some leaders. The leadership is there. If you go out and work with your people, then the leadership will emerge.... We don't know who they are now; we don't need to know. But the leadership will emerge from the movement that emerges.[12]

Although he held a graduate degree in mathematics from Harvard, Moses dressed in overalls and treated everyone—students, sharecroppers, sheriffs—with the same dignity and respect.

Instead of descending on a town and proclaiming themselves as its saviors, SNCC organizers began by participating in the life of the community. Organizer Lawrence Guyot gave an example of a typical approach:

> You don't alter the basic format that you walk into. Let's say you're riding past a picnic, and people are cutting watermelons. You don't immediately go and say, "Stop the watermelon cuttin', and let's talk about voter registration." You cut some watermelons, or you help somebody else serve 'em.[13]

Even though many of the SNCC staffers were outsiders, they lived in the same houses, wore the same clothes, and ate the same foods as the poor Southern blacks whom they organized. Amzie Moore, a community leader who left the NAACP for SNCC, was impressed that the "kids," unlike the affluent ministers who headed the other civil rights organizations,

> wore blue jeans, and I used to have sleeping in my house six and eight and ten, twelve, who had come. I bought a lot of cheese, and always we'd eat cheese and peaches, and sometimes we would get spaghetti and ground chuck or ground beef and make a huge tub of meatballs and spaghetti to fill everybody up.[14]

Despite the hardships, Casey Hayden, a white Southern SNCC staffer, remembers that "there was a comfort in that time that was born of the absolute certainty that what I was doing was the right thing to be doing."[15]

This respectful attitude toward people who expected to be despised helped them to take the first step toward what historian Lawrence Goodwyn has called "political self-respect."[17] But it was the SNCC workers' militancy, in the face of violence and other forms of harassment, which inspired Southern blacks to find the courage to act for themselves. Unita Blackwell, a Mississippian, remembers that

> Bob Moses was a little bitty fella. And he stood up to this sheriff and Bob said, "I'm from SNCC." I had never saw that

happen before. From that day on, I said, "Well, I can stand myself."[17]

Despite arrests, beatings, and murders, Blackwell and thousands of others "stood" themselves: marching, rallying, and engaging in nonviolent civil disobedience. Southern sheriffs and mayors, the official enforcers of segregation, had never before confronted a genuine popular movement. According to Amzie Moore,

> If 'leven people went to jail this evening who the power structure considered leaders, tomorrow morning you had 'leven more out there.... And the next morning 'leven more.[18]

In SNCC's view, the key to the transformation of the South was peaceful, mass disobedience of the "Jim Crow" laws, which required segregation in restaurants, on buses, and in other public places and facilities.

Nonviolence was both means and end, or as Lawson told the SNCC founding conference, "both judgment and promise."[19] Only individuals who truly understood and practiced nonviolence would be capable of democratic politics; only such individuals could bring into being a political democracy. SNCC's "Statement of Purpose" proclaimed: "By appealing to conscience and standing on the moral nature of human existence, nonviolence nurtures the atmosphere in which reconciliation and justice become real possibilities."[20] Nonviolence made reconciliation as well as justice possible by appealing to the consciences of those who supported injustice, actively or passively.

Drawing explicitly on Judeo Christian traditions, the "Statement" explained that

> Love is the central motif of nonviolence.... Such love goes to the extreme; it remains loving and forgiving even in the midst of hostility. It matches the capacity of evil to inflict suffering with an even more enduring capacity to absorb evil, all the while persisting in love.[21]

Compelled by nonviolence to face up to the contradiction between their consciences and their actions, white Southeners would be transformed into loving human beings ready to cast aside the evil of segregation. A confrontation between student leader Diane Nash and Mayor Ben West of Nashville during a march to support the lunch counter sit-ins illustrates the very real power of nonviolent action. After reading a prepared statement, Nash began to ask the mayor direct questions. C.T. Vivian, the march leader, remembers very clearly that

> I felt that the mayor wanted to answer with the normal political talk. But then the questions came: Are you against segregation? Are you for what is happening in this city? He looked out across the expanse of four thousand people and he said, "No, no, I'm not for it. I do not think racism is right," or words to the same effect.[22]

Diane Nash thinks she knows why the mayor changed his mind:

> I confronted Mayor West with what his feelings were as a man, as a person. I was particularly interested in that, as opposed to his just being a mayor. I have a lot of respect for the way he responded. He didn't have to respond the way he did. He said that he felt it was wrong for the citizens of Nashville to be discriminated against at the lunch counters solely on the basis of the color of their skin. That was the turning point. The Nashville newspaper reported his statement in the headlines the next day, and it was one more step toward desegregating the lunch counters.[23]

Nonviolence made it possible for Nash to address the mayor "as a person," which in turn compelled him to respond as one. She and the other protesters were no longer merely victims, just as he and the other whites were no longer merely victimizers.[24]

The redemptive community promised to redeem whites as well as blacks, by recovering for both the true American tradition of democracy. As Martin Luther King put it, in his influential "Letter From A Birmingham Jail,"

> One day the South will know that when these disinherited children of God sat down at the lunch counters, they were in reality standing up for what is best in the American dream and for the most sacred values in our Judeo-Christian heritage, thereby bringing the entire nation back to the wells of democracy that were dug deep by the founding fathers.[25]

King suggests that the best way to honor the memory of the founders is to stand up, as they did, for what is best in the American dream: democracy. The disinherited blacks participating in the civil rights movement understood the inheritance better than did the white Southern bigots. Even more than King's own organization, SNCC put into practice his vision of remembrance as action.

The high point of SNCC's effort to bring the nation back to the wells of democracy was the Mississippi Freedom Summer of 1964, directed by Bob Moses. Hundreds of Northern students, mostly white, came south to help SNCC organizers and local activists register voters, teach in Freedom Schools, develop self-help projects, including healthcare clinics and small-business cooperatives, and hold elections for the MFDP delegation to the Democratic convention. The Mississippi achievements inspired democratic action in other states, including the original Black Panther Party in Lowndes County, Alabama. Like its Mississippi cousin, the Alabama party conducted a voter registration drive and ran its own slate of candidates. The symbol of the black panther was chosen to make it easier for illiterate Southern blacks voting for the first time; instead of the Democratic donkey or the Republican elephant, they just pulled the level for the panther.

In addition to these successes at the grassroots, SNCC's unparalleled ability to organize people to participate in civil disobedience was indispensible to the success of the civil rights movement at the national level. The eloquence of Martin Luther King Jr., the most visible leader, was backed up by the militance of thousands of anonymous Southern blacks and their supporters, who risked jail and their lives for simple democracy. The pressure from below, combined with the political opening following the assassination of John F. Kennedy, made possible the passage of the 1964 Civil Rights Act. This historic act outlawed discrimination, not merely on the basis of color or race, but also national origin, religion, and sex, in voting, employment, public places, and any programs receiving funding from the federal government. In 1965, the Voting Rights Act removed the remaining barriers to the free exercise of the right to vote, including the poll tax.

But these victories came at a high price. The murders of three civil rights workers during Freedom Summer confirmed that white supremacists were willing to use all means, legal and illegal, peaceful and violent, to maintain their power. Frustrated SNCC staffers debated whether their commitments to nonviolence and interracialism were holding the movement back. Was it a waste of time to try to build participatory institutions before the existing ones had been dismantled?

The increased national attention that SNCC drew raised further issues. Could the strategies that were so successful against legal discrimination in the rural South be applied to the more intractable social and economic problems of the urban North? And could the media's preference for charismatic leaders and photogenic action be reconciled with SNCC's commitment to leaderless politics and slow, undramatic grassroots organizing?

In late 1964, Bob Moses changed his last name to his mother's maiden name, Parris, in a vain attempt to thwart the tendency of reporters, as well as SNCC staff and supporters, to treat him as the leader, a veritable "Moses." For the same reason, he soon resigned his position as the director of the coalition formed by SNCC and other civil rights groups to organize in Mississippi. Moses's decisions suggest the difficulty of practicing participatory politics, even within a small group of committed activists.

For one thing, SNCC's rejection of leaders did not eliminate people's need or desire for them, as a Freedom Summer volunteer noted after Moses's resignation:

> Bob's case illustrates one of the real problems of the anti-leadership style of organization. His opinion was eagerly sought because of his experience and the faith people had in his ability and knowledge. When he refused to give it, knowing that it would carry considerable authority, the group was deprived of valuable counsel and sometimes spent great amounts of time trying to figure out what Bob really wanted, since he refused to say.[26]

Unlike Moses, many organizers felt torn between their commitment to participatory democracy and their recognition that, in certain situations, they *did* know better than the people whom they were organizing. For Lawrence Guyot, "the most painful lesson for some of us was how to let [the organization] go once you've set it into motion."[27] Because inexperienced leaders inevitably made mistakes, an SNCC manual warned that the organizer should not "let the project go to the dogs because you feel that you must be democratic to the letter or carry out every parliamentary procedure."[28]

And it was not easy to be democratic to the letter, even when you tried to be. Only full-time organizers could be members of SNCC; very few people, generally students without families or other commitments, could devote themselves to the twenty-four-hour-a-day experiment in democracy. This inevitably created distance between the organizers and the organized, which was widened by the fact that so many of the students—Northern, urban, middle class, and white— were entering the rural South for the first time.

Moreover, some "brothers" in the band were more equal than others, while the brothers as a group were superior to the "sisters." In 1964, staffers Mary King and Casey Hayden circulated an anonymous memo complaining that "the woman in SNCC is often in the same position as that token Negro hired in a corporation."[29] Almost everyone complained, at some time or other, about the effort required to make decisions by consensus; meetings went on late into the night as exhausted organizers struggled to reach agreement. Perhaps, their frustration was exacerbated by unrealistic expectations that brothers and sisters will never disagree, that participatory democracy requires unanimity, or that "this American democracy" could be quickly transformed.

The redemption of a relatively few Southern blacks and whites did not result in the redemption of many of their communities, let alone the South as a whole. The victories of the early sixties triggered resistance, making it still harder to sustain the commitment to participatory democracy. Even Bob Moses showed the strain from years of struggle. Connie Curry, a SNCC worker, recalls that

> It just made him into a...—it just broke his heart. And the reaction to that—there's something in the Irish rebellion that says, "A heart broken too often turns to stone." He used to get hurt everytime anybody would look mean at him, literally. I mean, he would feel it, and you could imagine that kind of sensitivity in Mississippi where people wanted to kill him.[30]

Many SNCC members came to have doubts, not only about whether democracy could be achieved, but about whether the people even wanted or deserved it. In 1963, four black teenage girls were killed during the bombing of a Birmingham church, only two weeks after the dramatic March on Washington which featured King's "I have a dream" speech. Anne Moody, a sharecropper's daughter from rural Mississippi who had joined SNCC, recalls her first reaction: if "Martin

Luther King thinks nonviolence is really going to work for the South as it did for India, then he is out of his mind." The problem, as Moody saw it, was not merely those segregationists who would do anything to stop the movement, but also the majority of the blacks, who

> were afraid to walk the streets. When they passed the office, they turned their heads to keep from looking in. Every time I passed one of them on the street, they looked at me and almost said, "Get out of here. You'll get us killed."[31]

Yet, the following Wednesday, nearly two hundred blacks gathered outside the office to receive the free clothes that SNCC was giving away. Moody remembers:

> The minute I saw them there, I got mad as hell. "Here they are," I thought, "all standing around waiting to be given something. Last week after the church bombing they turned their heads when they passed this office. Some even looked at me with hate in their eyes. Now they are smiling at me. After I give them the clothes, they probably won't even look at me next week, let alone go and register to vote."[32]

In response to such frustrating experiences, SNCC split into two factions during the fall of 1964.[33] The "freedom highs," who modeled themselves after Bob Moses, favored continuing to develop grassroots movements and leadership. The "structure faction," led by James Forman, argued for a more centralized structure that could support SNCC's increasingly national activities:

No one is questioning the fact that everybody within SNCC is a decision-maker.... In this respect we have been different from other organizations that attempted to control decisions made by staff people in the field from a central point. On the other hand, that freedom to make decisions has created many problems and strains within the organization.

I call for internal cohesion.... We must continue, not necessarily to work for the redemptive society, but to work toward a new spirit of brotherhood, a spirit that transcends both black and white, a spirit that supersedes, a spirit that goes above and a spirit that sees all of us simply as men and women, struggling for a sense of dignity.... We must decide if the circle will be unbroken.[34]

Bob Moses's response was to ask, "Do we build an SNCC machine...or do we organize the people?"[35]

In February 1965, following a period of internal turmoil, the structure faction won; local organizing in the South gave way to publicity campaigns focused on the problems of the urban North. SNCC also adopted a separatist approach, expelling its white members; as Executive Secretary Stokely Carmichael put it, "We can not have the oppressors telling the oppressed how to rid themselves of the oppressor."[36] Even Bob Moses, who had led the fight to include white students in Freedom Summer because "I always thought that the one thing we can do for the country that no one else can do is to be above the race issue," announced that he was breaking off all relationships with whites.[37]

As its national stature grew, SNCC became identified

no longer with participatory democracy, but with its charismatic spokesmen for Black Power, especially Stokely Carmichael and H. Rap Brown. An SNCC leaflet, produced in Chicago during the summer riots of 1967, expressed the later philosophy of the organization:

> We must fill ourselves with hate for all white things. This is not vengeance or trying to take the white oppressors' place to become new black oppressors but is a oneness with a worldwide black brotherhood....
>
> We must stop fighting a "fair game." We must do whatever is necessary to win BLACK POWER. We have to hate and disrupt and destroy and blackmail and lie and steal and become blood-brothers like the Mau-Mau.[38]

In contrast to SNCC's original "Statement of Purpose," this leaflet substitutes hate for love, which is now seen as nothing more than a hopeless, humiliating effort "to beg the white man."[39] Instead of looking to the Constitution or other American democratic traditions, Chicago SNCC calls on blacks to identify with a worldwide black brotherhood of the oppressed against the white oppressors.

In 1966, in a popular essay entitled "The Angry Children of Malcolm X," SNCC staffer Julius Lester announced that

> America has had chance after chance to show that it really meant "that all men are endowed with certain inalienable rights." America has had precious chances in this decade to make it come true. Now it is over. The days of singing freedom

> songs and the days of combatting bullets and billy clubs with
> love.... Now they sing: Too much love,/ Too much love,/
> Nothing kills a nigger like too much love.[40]

Lester's title seems to be a direct reference to Martin Luther King, Jr.'s "disinherited children of God," in the "Letter From A Birmingham Jail." When that letter was written in 1963, the civil rights movement was proud to stand for "what is best in the American dream," democracy. Just a few years later, many activists believed that it was counterproductive to invoke America's so-called democratic tradition. As Malcolm X himself put it: "what to them is an American dream to us is an American nightmare."[41]

By this time, King himself was expressing ambivalence about the American dream. In 1968, shortly before his assasination, he suggested that the founding fathers had left a negative legacy, too:

> There is an Old Testament prophecy of the "sins of the Fathers
> being visited upon the third and fourth generations." Nothing
> could be more applicable to our situation. America is reaping
> the harvest of hate and shame planted through generations of
> educational denial, political dis-enfranchisement and
> economic exploitation of its black population. Now, almost a
> century removed from slavery, we find the heritage of
> oppression and racism erupting in our cities, with volcanic lava
> of bitterness and frustration pouring down our avenues.[42]

These reflections on the dual heritage of America were written during King's final project, the Poor

People's Campaign. His increasing pessimism was a reaction to the frustrations of trying to shift his movement's focus from the South to the North, and from legalized segregation to the poverty that crossed racial and geographic lines.

SNCC's turn toward the North was similarly frustrated. Unable to organize a popular base as it had in the South, the group split again into two factions, the cultural nationalists and the political revolutionaries, both of which soon fell apart. As Program Secretary Cleveland Sellers put it, "while Establishment leaders denounced our spreading influence, we were doing everything possible to keep our organization from collapsing."[43]

Meanwhile, some of the Freedom Summer volunteers and expelled white members had gone on to participate in the second great sixties experiment in participatory democracy, the ERAP project of the Students for a Democratic Society.

"An Interracial Movement of the Poor"

The Economic Research and Action Project (ERAP) was the major effort of the Students for a Democratic Society to practice participatory politics.[44]

SDS, the most visible organization of the New Left, was founded in 1962 in Port Huron, Michigan, by white college students whose prospects were far better than their parents' (and later, their childrens'). Born during the period of affluence following World War II, the baby boomers could count on good salaries, job security, owning suburban homes with two-car garages, and affordable educations. In their influential manifesto, "The Port Huron Statement," they described themselves: "We are people of this generation, bred in at least modest comfort, housed in universities, looking uncomfortably to the world we inherit."[45]

Politically, the SDS was uncomfortable with a democratic tradition that included them, but excluded others. Like their counterparts in SNCC, they were determined to take action to close the gap between the ideal and the reality of American politics. In the "Statement," they put into writing what SNCC had put into practice:

> As a social system we seek the establishment of a democracy of individual participation, governed by two central aims: that the individual share in those social decisions determining the quality and direction of his life; that society be organized to encourage independence in men and provide the media for their common participation.[46]

This passage was condensed into the popular slogan that became SDS's signature, "participatory democracy." The Port Huron Statement itself was produced through a participatory process. Drafted by Tom Hayden, a student journalist from the University of Michigan, the Statement was debated, revised, and finally ratified on June 16, 1962, by all fifty-nine activists who attended the founding convention.

But, for all its power as a slogan, the precise meaning of participatory democracy was not very clear. Sharon Jeffrey, one of the original ratifiers of The Port Huron Statement had been raised by activist parents who took her to her first picket line at the age of five. Jeffrey recalls that she had a "very personalized sense of participatory democracy":

> "Participatory" meant "involved in decisions." And I definitely wanted to be involved in decisions that were going to affect me! How could I let anyone make a decision about me that I wasn't involved in? The other sentence [in The Port Huron Statement] that is essential to me is "The goal of man in society should be human independence, finding a meaning of life that is authentic." I think authenticity is something that we were deeply committed to discovering within ourselves. I had a very personalized sense of participatory democracy—but I could also connect it to black students, I could connect it to students in universities, I could connect it to the Third World.[47]

But, couldn't someone in these categories have a different understanding of participatory democracy than Jeffrey? How can disputes among people with conflicting personalized senses of participatory democracy be resolved? But, like their counterparts in SNCC, the enthusiastic young SDS members preferred action to analysis. In fact, too much theory could be dangerous, as a flyer explained: "ideology disunites, action unites."[48]

In his influential novel, *The Armies of the Night*, Norman Mailer captured the activist spirit of the New Left, as he observed it during the 1967 March on the Pentagon:

> You created the revolution first and learned from it.... [T]he future of the revolution existed in the nerves and cells of the people who created it and lived with it, rather than the sanctity of the original idea.[49]

The Economic Research and Action Project was inspired by SNCC's success at community organizing in the South, at a time when Northern student activists felt increasingly marginalized on campus. Many SDS members, including its first president, Tom Hayden, had experienced the SNCC approach firsthand. In 1963, Hayden wrote:

> Can the methods of SNCC be applied to the North?... Can we spread our organizational power as far as our ideological influence, or are we inevitably assigned to a vague educational role in a society that increasingly is built deaf to the sounds of protest?[50]

In response to SNCC's evolving position that whites should work in white communities, SDS decided to organize among the Northern, white, urban poor. The student activists hoped to eventually join with SNCC and other groups organizing in black communities to build "an interracial movement of the poor."[51]

Significantly, ERAP was only adopted after contentious debate. Al Haber, the original director, asked: "Is radicalism subsisting in a slum for a year or two, or is it developing your individual talents so you can function as a radical in your professional field and throughout your adult life?"[52] The excitement of finally getting out into the community overwhelmed Haber's implied prediction that college students would not find it so easy to organize people very different from themselves. ERAP began in September 1963 with a five-thousand-dollar grant from the United Auto Workers Union. Teams of organizers were sent off to several cities, including Newark, Chicago, and Cleveland, each team dedicated "to the development of a community organization capable of achieving a better deal for the poor in a democratic fashion."[53]

Like the members of SNCC, the ERAP activists were committed to creating and modeling, within their own organizations, the participatory democracy which they hoped to achieve in the cities and eventually in the nations. "Let the people decide," a slogan borrowed from SNCC, expressed ERAP's approach to community organizing. The organizers attempted to imitate SNCC's "image of the organizer who never organized, who by his simple presence was the mystical medium for the spontaneous expression of the people."[54] In fact, ERAP tried to go even further, to eliminate leadership altogether. As a member of the community organization in Newark said,

We don't believe in leadership. We believe in one man, one vote. We have a program committee meeting once a week. All our blocks that we have organized come together at the program committee meeting. We discuss each problem that occurs on our blocks and let the people decide what kind of action they want to take to solve the problem.... We have rotating chairmen who serve four weeks and then are replaced by the program committee.

We in NCUP do not believe in leadership because so many organizations have been sold out by leaders.[55]

The ERAP organizing teams adopted the SNCC model of living and working together in the neighborhoods which they were trying to organize. A journalist reported that the students in NCUP

are not down there for a visit to the slums. They are part of the slums, a kind of lay-brotherhood, or worker-priests, except that they have no dogma to sell. They get no salary; they live on a subsistence allowance that the project as a whole uses for rent or food.... They eat a spartan diet of powdered milk and large quantities of peanut butter and jelly, which seems to be the SDS staple.[56]

Within their teams, the ERAP organizers tried to attain the SNCC model of a band of brothers, standing in a circle of love. ERAP members tried to live the analogy drawn by one New Leftist, that the

extraordinary intimacy experienced by people who have fallen in love is akin to that felt by more participation in great political movements: one's sensory world expands, becomes more intense, the boundaries between people

> become diffused, ordinary human selfishness is replaced by
> an unusual altruism....[57]

The young organizers' willingness to practice not merely preach participatory democracy had the same transforming impact on some of the poor Northerners, as on some of the Southern blacks. A community member in Chicago JOIN (Jobs or Income Now) described his personal experience of participation:

> [W]ith ERAP I feel more dedicated than when I started 'cause things are starting to happen and I was partly responsible for buildin' things that happened....You get a great feeling when you see a group of people standin' around demanding stuff that is rightfully theirs. I mean it's theirs and they never had it before and they want it now. It makes me feel good that after a year and a half the neighborhood has changed like that.... So I can't drop out now, 'cause for one thing I don't want to. Things are in such a state where you have to fight 'em through and maybe eventually come up with an organization of people who control the community.[58]

As in SNCC, members of ERAP believed that transformed individuals would transform their communities into ones controlled by the people who lived in them.

At its peak, ERAP had projects in ten cities, with a total of approximately 300 staff members. These projects achieved important victories: in Cleveland, ERAP organized a group of poor white women into Citizens United For Adequate Welfare (CUFAW), which won a free lunch program for poor children in the city schools; in Newark, ERAP founded the Newark Community Union Project (NCUP), which conducted several successful rent strikes, improved garbage collection, and got a play street established; in Chicago, ERAP won concessions from the local employment and welfare offices; in Chester, Pennsylvania, with the help of Swarthmore College students, ERAP built a strong community organization that successfully attacked racial discrimination.

Despite these often temporary gains, the ERAP organizers ultimately failed to achieve their vision of democracy in the world around them, or even to live it themselves. Compared to SNCC, which did succeed in establishing, if not sustaining community organizations, ERAP barely got off the ground. Even more than their SNCC role models, ERAP staffers were outsiders entering communities greatly different from their own. Moreover, unemployment, their main issue, was actually decreasing as a result of the widening Vietnam War. The Northern poor who were still unable to find jobs in a stronger economy were much more isolated, demoralized, and difficult to organize than the Southern rural blacks who drew strength from comparatively vibrant local communities and institutions, particularly their churches.

Within the organizations founded by ERAP, the practice of participatory democracy fell short of the ideal. Despite the slogan, the people often *did not* decide. Todd Gitlin, an SDS president and ERAP organizer, recalls that

> the self-abnegating style of participatory democracy didn't eliminate leadership, only disguised it. The de facto leaders were still influential; followers were swayed willy-nilly. Diffident leaders in disguise couldn't be held accountable, and ended up more manipulative than when they stood up tall, made their authority explicit, presented solid targets.[59]

An experience of Sharon Jeffrey's in Cleveland illustrates the problem of disguised leadership, even when there is no deliberate attempt at manipulation. At one of the first meetings of CUFW, the welfare rights organization organized by ERAP, a minister proposed a symbolic "stealing campaign." At a nearby department store, the group would protest against poverty by openly "stealing" a token piece of clothing. After a lively debate, the members of the organization, mostly single mothers on welfare, agreed on the plan. Yet, following this apparently successful instance of participatory democracy,

> Jeffrey and her colleagues made a sobering discovery. The mothers hadn't grasped the symbolism of the tactic. They thought that the group was actually going to steal— surreptitiously—badly needed clothes. Several of the women, considering themselves upright and honest, had been upset by the idea. Intimidated by the articulateness of the organizers, they had kept their misgivings to themselves. What had seemed like an organizing breakthrough had been a fiasco.[60]

Based on his experiences in Chicago JOIN, Richie Rothstein concluded that the slogan, "let the people decide," encouraged "the organizers to pretend (at the time even to themselves) that 'the people' were deciding issues that only organizers knew about, let alone understood."[61]

Even when the organizers were genuinely committed to letting the people decide, it could be just as difficult as it had been for SNCC. How many people, other than the organizers themselves, had the time available for democratic participation? In an unconvincing effort to portray the slowness of participatory decision making in a more positive light, an ERAP pamphlet proclaimed: "Freedom is an endless meeting."[62]

Like Anne Moody, some ERAP organizers concluded that the people did not necessarily want this kind of freedom, did not want to decide. One staff member groused,

> I go out every so often and be friendly (which is often quite pleasant) and listen to people complain and say that they don't have time to do anything and that you can't do anything and that they are moving, and that the neighbors and the kids are bastards. Shit.[63]

However, another organizer, Nick Egelson, had a different explanation for the apparent apathy. Perhaps people were simply too smart to take great risks for the mere pretense of democracy: "if they fail, they get fired, if they win, they still have to work at the same stuff and live in almost the same way: they won't be much better off." In Egelson's view, the poor residents of Hoboken didn't join ERAP "because they perceive the smallness of the organization compared to the enormity of the problem much better than we...do."[64]

Within the organizing teams, participatory democracy also proved difficult to practice. As in SNCC, some organizers were more equal than others. Men dominated ERAP, even though women were usually the most successful organizers (in part, because they were sent to work with the women of the community who were easier to organize during this period than the chronically unemployed men).[65]

Still, ERAP came much closer to realizing participatory democracy on the inside of the organization than on the outside. Jeffrey recalls:

> A lot of our experimentation was on a personal level. We got enthralled by ourselves and our own group process. That became more important than any other issue.[66]

In the phrase of Carol McEldowney, also with Cleveland ERAP, the organizers focused on the relationships among themselves to such an extent that "participatory democracy came to mean all-night staff sessions that sounded like group therapy."[67]

However, even redefined in this way, participatory democracy failed to maintain the group, let alone change the world. In Cleveland, McEldowney split up with her husband, Ken, an event that "was really shocking to all of us," according to Jeffrey:

> How could this be? How could our happy family be deluded? If they weren't getting along, how is it that we didn't know?"[68]

Mounting frustrations led to an ERAP-wide debate over a more effective strategy for community organizing. Like SNCC, the ERAP staffers divided into two camps, JOIN and GROIN ("Garbage Removal or Income Now").[69] JOIN emphasized broad issues requiring a fundamental transformation of society, while GROIN focused on the local problems which seemed most urgent to the people of a given community. The GROIN approach was somewhat more successful, since concrete results such as garbage removal attracted new members to the organization. However, community members tended to drift away when the organizers found it difficult, in the absence of a national movement for social change, to keep delivering even small victories.

By 1965, almost all of the ERAP projects had been shut down. The organizers had only rarely been able to establish strong community organizations, nor did the few successes add up to anything like an interracial movement of the poor.

In fact, ERAP succumbed to many of the same problems that frustrated SNCC in its move from South to North, especially the intractability of economic and social inequalities compared to legalized discrimination, complicated by co-optation and repression. Many of the most talented community leaders were offered jobs in the new government anti-poverty programs that ERAP had helped to bring about, while the few efforts at more radical action were easily crushed. At the same time, the escalating Vietnam War directed SDS's attention back toward the campuses. Organizing students against the war came to seem more urgent than continuing the frustrating ERAP.

The antiwar marches which SDS organized in Washington, D.C., attracted thousands of people, and received massive attention from the media. (The first speaker at the first march, on April 17, 1965, was Bob Parris, as he was then known, who compared the killing of the Vietnamese to the murders of the civil rights workers in Mississippi). Thousands of students also joined SDS, which became the most visible antiwar organization on the national scene. The movement against the Vietnam War had an unprecedented impact on American politics, influencing President Lyndon Johnson's decision not to seek a second term, and, eventually, contributing to the end of the war.

However, the sudden influx of new members during the late sixties changed the character of the organization, from a small group of activists trying to implement participatory democracy to a mass movement with a loose structure and an increasingly ideological core of nominal leaders. Although the decentralized movement offered many opportunities to experiment with participatory politics, SDS itself became less and less democratic. In 1969, only four years after organizing the first national protest against the war, SDS disintegrated, "splintering into several warring factions, each claiming to be more revolutionary than thou."[70] Like SNCC, SDS achieved its greatest national recognition only after leaving behind its early commitment to participatory democracy.

Although a few of the ERAP staffers returned to community organizing (Sharon Jeffrey became director of the Hyde Park-Kenwood Community Conference in Chicago), most found it difficult to carry on as full-time activists during the polarized, turbulent late sixties. A tiny few swore allegiance to revolutionary sects such as the ones which took over SDS. Other former staffers continued their experimentation on the personal level, in the counterculture.

For some, their experiences in community organizing, the antiwar movement, or the counterculture produced "a growing sense of being outlaws in America."[71] A few, like Cathy Wilkerson, literally became outlaws, engaging in terrorist acts and then spending years underground or in jail. Even those who continued to work for social change gradually abandoned their hopes of recovering the "true democracy" in America.

"This American Democracy"

Fannie Lou Hamer's journey from the cotton fields to the Democratic National Party Convention exemplifies both the success and the failure of the sixties experiments in participatory democracy. Through SNCC, Hamer moved from acquiesence to participation, but not all the way to power.

The twentieth child in a family of sharecroppers, Hamer began picking cotton at the age of six. Until SNCC organizers came to her town, she never questioned the fact that blacks were not allowed to take part in elections. In 1962, when she tried to register to vote, the owner of the cotton plantation where she had worked and lived for years fired her and evicted the Hamer family from their company home. At the Democratic convention, Fannie Lou Hamer testified that the police had beaten her with a blackjack for attending a civil rights meeting: "I screamed to God in pain. My dress worked itself up. I tried to pull it down. They beat my arms 'til I had no feeling in them." Weeping, she asked the delegates and a national television audience: "Is this America? The land of the free and the home of the brave?"[72]

But the convention was controlled by President Lyndon Johnson, who feared antagonizing Southern Democrats; so, he arranged a "compromise" in which only two members of the MFDP would be seated, along with the entire regular delegation. The MFDP protested in vain; Hamer told reporters that the two seats represented "token seats on the back row, the same as we got in Mississippi." Bob Moses added "I will have nothing to do with the political system any longer."[73]

Despite their failure to transform American democracy, the sixties movements made a difference. Their most visible achievements were helping to end legal discrimination in the South and to stop the Vietnam War. But their most important legacy has been largely hidden: the vision and experience of participatory politics that influenced the feminist, gay and lesbian, environmental, and peace movements of the seventies and eighties, and which remains alive, if often unrecognized, in local community organizing today.

THREE

REMEMBERING THE SIXTIES

ON February 21, 1993, Bob Moses was the subject of a cover story in the *New York Times Magazine*. The cover itself was a full-page photograph of Moses teaching mathematics to Mississippi Delta children, with the headline, "We Shall Overcome, This Time With Algebra."

Inside, the article informs us that, in Mississippi during the sixties, Moses was respected as "the equivalent of Martin Luther King."[1] Now, "after years of self-imposed exile, the civil rights legend is back, fighting the same war with a new weapon."[2]

The new weapon is algebra; as director of the Algebra Project, dedicated to improving the math education of the poor, Moses has been, in the phrase of the reporter, "retooled for the 90s." In Moses's words,

> It's our version of Civil Rights 1992.... The question we asked then was: What are the skills people have to master to open the doors to citizenship? Now math literacy holds the key.[3]

As sincere as Moses seems to be, it is hard not to wonder how math literacy can replace the key to citizenship for which Moses and SNCC fought during the sixties: the right to participate fully in politics. Yet, this lengthy article, on the man who exemplified the idea that "we are all leaders," almost erases the memory of SNCC and participatory democracy. Instead, the *Times* tells a generic story of a young radical who grew up, setting aside childish politics for a career which promises to improve the lives of individuals without threatening the unequal distribution of power. At most, Moses's students may be better able to calculate the widening gap between their own incomes and those of the rich.

The image of the "retooled" sixties activist-turned-math-teacher illustrates the way in which our memories of the democratic movements of the sixties both shape and reflect the politics of the nineties. In a period of declining political participation, the resurgence of interest in the sixties has largely ignored the positive experiences of participatory democracy within the civil rights movement and the New Left. Although our national memory is contested, the dominant, negative story we tell ourselves about the sixties discourages participatory politics today.

"Flying and Falling Through the 60s"

Shortly after the 1991 Gulf War, the *New York Times* devoted the front page of its Living Arts section almost entirely to the sixties. A huge photograph dominates the page; it is actor Val Kilmer portraying rock star Jim Morrison strutting with a microphone in *The Doors*. The headline is "Flying and Falling Through the 60s: A Life of the Doors." Below the fold is a picture of two actors portraying crazed Vietnam veterans, from a new play about the legacy of the war; the headline is "*Speed of Darkness* Turns Back the Clock for a Nation and a Family." The third and smallest picture is the sole exception to the sixties theme; it shows a shrapnel-punctured helmet from a World War I battle. The article beneath describes a visit to the West Point Museum, which left the reporter feeling "strangely serene."[4]

Taken as a whole, the page serves as a visual representation of the sixties used as a metaphor. It contrasts our true past—the periodic reunification of our national family through war, as symbolized by the serene weapons displayed at West Point—with the false past of psychotic Vietnam vets and hedonistic rock stars, emblems of the flying, falling, dark sixties. The title of the recent book, *Years of Discord: American Politics and Society, 1961–1974*, by the noted historian John Morton Blum, neatly sums up the negative interpretation of the period as the most divisive in our history.[5]

To refer negatively to the sixties in political discourse is to call up memories of young people in revolt: disheveled, wild-eyed demonstrators rioting in the streets of Chicago during the 1968 Democratic National Party Convention; Black Panthers in leather and berets, carrying rifles and shouting "Black Power!"; a noisy group of unkempt, unshaved women burning their bras during the Miss America Pageant; hundreds of thousands of unkempt, unshaved, and naked young people making love and taking drugs in the open air, while rock groups play ear-shatteringly loud music with unintelligible or obscene lyrics at Woodstock. By evoking such images, the dominant sixties-as-metaphor tells the cautionary tale of a childish rebellion against America.

Peter Collier and David Horowitz, for instance, are self-described "second thoughters," former members of the New Left who now see their sixties cohorts as a "destructive generation."[6] The best-selling authors, former editors of *Ramparts* magazine, admit that "what we called politics in the Sixties was exactly what...many of our political elders tried to say it was before we shouted them down—an Oedipal revolt on a grand scale." Sigmund Freud used the ancient Greek story of Oedipus, the king who unwittingly killed his father and married his mother, to illustrate his theory that every young boy secretly wishes to rebel against and to replace his own father. But, in Collier and Horowitz's version of the Oedipal revolt, the elders have the last word. Oedipus is defeated, realizes his error, and attends conferences in which he and other members of a "radical generation talk about finally coming home again."[7]

In content as well as style, the second thoughters resemble the former Old Leftists who recanted during the fifties, and went on to become the harshest critics of the movement to which they had once belonged. In both cases, the former "true believers" have reached a wide audience by stating explicitly the views underlying more moderate versions of political discourse. Nearly all of them are white men focusing on the movement that was dominated by white men, the New Left. The civil rights movement is almost invisible in the negative story of the sixties, except for the images of gun-wielding Panthers and "unqualified" blacks demanding affirmative action in order to steal white men's jobs.

In the dominant sixties-as-metaphor, the idea of participatory democracy was at best, unimportant. The index to John Morton Blum's book, for instance, contains no listing for "participatory democracy." At best, the slogan was mere camouflage for totalitarianism or chaos. As the conservative philosopher Allan Bloom put it, "Whether it be Nuremberg or Woodstock, the principle is the same."[8] What could be the common principle behind the Nazi state and the anarchic counterculture? Opposition to genuine democracy, in which the people rule by electing their superiors to rule over them.

Bloom's diatribe against the influence of the sixties on higher education, *The Closing of the American Mind*, was a surprising best-seller, which suggests that the negative sixties-as-metaphor appeals to a far greater audience than merely disgruntled classicists, or former radicals with axes to grind. *Our Country: The Shaping of America from Roosevelt to Reagan*, by Michael Barone, a senior writer for *U.S. News and World Report*, was another best-seller featuring a strong attack on the sixties. Although his analysis is more moderate than Bloom's, or Collier's and Horowitz's, Barone distinguishes sharply between the reforms he applauds, such as the expansion of civil rights, and the student activists

> whose complaints reeked of adolescent angst.... These were the cries of elite adolescents angry and bewildered that they

had not, at twenty-one, gained the powers of their elders,
quite reached the top levels of society.[9]

Fortunately, in the negative story of the sixties, the
dangerous movements were defeated, and the
American way of life and politics restored. Responsible
maturity triumphed over whining adolescence, orderly
politics over unruly action, and genuine democracy
over its fraudulent participatory cousin. To Barone, the
country "that emerged confident from years of turmoil
and stayed resilient after years of alienation, seemed
increasingly to be a model others wanted to follow, a
country that belonged not just to the many different
kinds of Americans but to peoples all over the world."[10]
And if some other nations seem to reject our model,
well, they just have not grown up and out of the sixties,
as the popular conservative humorist P. J. O'Rourke
explains:

> Third World countries are undergoing national adolescences
> very similar to the personal adolescence I underwent in the
> 60s. Woodstock Nation isn't dead; it's just become short,
> brown, distant and filled with chaos and starvation.... We are a
> beautiful woman and they are a wildly infatuated thirteen-
> year-old boy.... If they can't have a chance to love us, a chance
> to pester us will do—by joining the Soviet bloc for example.
> Anything for attention.[11]

In the wake of the collapse of the Soviet bloc, it
would seem that there is nothing left to shake our
confidence. Yet the proponents of the dominant sixties-

as-metaphor are surprisingly defensive. Despite the defeat of the sixties movements and the rejection of liberal politics during the seventies and the eighties, conservatives and neoconservatives still view their opponents as an imminent threat. To Collier and Horowitz, the left resembles a horror film monster about to devour us if we relax our vigilance: "Like the slowly metamorphosing monster of a horror film, the Left has actually been recreating itself during its apparent dormancy since the end of the Sixties, succeeding so well that now it has reappeared stronger than ever."[12]

How did the sixties monster recreate itself? By shifting the battlefield from politics to culture. Irving Kristol, a prominent former Old Leftist, had his second thoughts over thirty-five years ago. Now, Kristol sees a parallel between the tactics of the fifties Communists and their most recent spiritual descendents:

> This is the problem we have now, not with politics but with the culture. We non-radicals can keep winning elections, we keep winning elections, what good does it do us? A little bit of good, no doubt, but in the end the basic temper and mood is what dominates the novels, the poetry, the painting, the movies, all the things that affect our cultural life and all of the things that eventually shape our educational system and shape the minds and souls of our children.[13]

And who is in charge of our cultural and educational institutions? The supposedly defeated sixties radicals. In higher education, as in our culture as a whole, the apparent collapse of the sixties movements turns out to be a dangerous illusion. According to Roger Kimball, best known for his book, *Tenured Radicals: How Politics Has Corrupted Our Higher Education*, the "radical ethos of the sixties has been all too successful, achieving indirectly in the classroom, faculty meeting, and by administrative decree what it was unable to accomplish on the barricades."[14] On the defensive, the first and second thoughters accuse their opponents of "smelly little orthodoxies," "intellectual barbarisms," "diseases," including "spiritual immune deficiency," "cowardice," "playing the 'victim,'" and so on.[15]

Ironically, those who welcome a sixties revival see it as much less powerful than those who fear it.

"A Renewed Sense Of Hope"?

On November 22, 1992, the 29th anniversary of the assassination of President John F. Kennedy, the editorial section of the *Philadelphia Inquirer* featured a long article by Harris Wofford, then Senator from Pennsylvania and former member of Kennedy's staff. Although the title, "What Kennedys and King can teach us in the 90s," refers also to John's brother, Robert, and to Martin Luther King, the layout emphasizes the fallen President. Two columns of text surround a large drawing of three frames from a movie reel, a vertical sequence of Presidential heads. The middle frame is the only one that we see in its entirety; even this frame cannot contain all of John Kennedy's profile, which exudes the youthful optimism that is, to Wofford, the essence of the sixties:

> For many of us, 1992 feels a bit like 1960. Not only because of the superficial similarities of youth and vigor which Bill Clinton and John Kennedy share, but also because both of their elections generated a renewed sense of hope for change and action.[16]

Yet, Wofford also recognizes that, for many of his readers, it was all downhill after 1960. Hopes were dashed as change and action came to look like chaos and anarchy. So, before presenting his positive view of the decade, Wofford attempts to defuse the negative memory of the sixties that dominates American politics. He introduces this serious piece commemorating the assassination of a President with a scene from a classic movie, *The African Queen*. It's World War I in Africa, and Katharine Hepburn insists to a skeptical German naval captain that she and Humphrey Bogart really did travel down a supposedly unnavigable river in order to torpedo his war ship. Wofford's readers, at least those over forty, are likely to remember that just as the two stars are about to be hung, the German ship crashes into the floating torpedo, and Katharine and Humphrey swim off happily into the sunset. Wofford's article then formally begins: "It was a long river, with too many rapids and the passage was too fast, yet for all the wrong turns and terrible mistakes, the 60s were an extraordinary time of social invention and constructive politics."[17]

Does this odd, defensive strategy work? Not very well. Wofford's reference is probably mystyfying to any of today's youth who happen upon his article. And the essay itself, despite his intentions, testifies to the destructive politics of the period. Wofford's claim that the sixties have much to teach us is undercut by the fact that all three of his exemplary teachers were murdered. The illustration contributes to the discouraging tone; it is a deliberate reference to the famous Zapruder tape of the Kennedy assassination, which had just been brought again to the public's attention by the Oliver Stone film, *JFK*. Wofford's own attempt to use film to establish his authority appears to backfire; his positive interpretation of the sixties seems like a sweet fantasy, as entertaining but insubstantial as *The African Queen*.

To refer sympathetically to the sixties in political discourse is to swim against the tide of American politics. The sixties-as-positive-metaphor tries to celebrate youthful activism in the name of participatory democracy, by calling up countermemories: blacks and whites marching peacefully behind Martin Luther King, past snarling police dogs, carrying signs that call for an end to segregation; a young man burning his draft card during a demonstration, risking his future to protest an unjust war; a group of women confessing to each other during a consciousness-raising group, each realizing for the first time that what she thought was a personal problem is really shared and political; thousands of young people dancing peacefully to the music of a new age at Woodstock.

In the positive use of the sixties as a metaphor, the participants in the New Left and the civil rights movement were not childish rebels against their country, but patriots dedicated to recovering and extending the American democratic tradition. As former student activist Jackie Goldberg recalls,

> We were the opposite of alienated and cynical. We believed in [America] so much that we were willing to take risks.[18]

Like Goldberg and Wofford, many of those who look favorably on the sixties are former or current activists. Their memoirs, and the histories written by scholars sympathetic to activism, help to clarify the views underlying the occasional positive references to the sixties that reach a wide audience. However, as sociologist Wini Breines has noted, the recent books which have received the most attention were written by well-known, former SDS leaders, including Todd Gitlin and Tom Hayden. Their influence may explain the emphasis in the positive sixties-as-metaphor on SDS and on the early sixties, the period in which these authors were the recognized leaders of the New Left.[19]

Although there have been several fine studies and memoirs of the civil rights movement, these have had much less impact on political discourse than the works by and about the young white male radicals. The excellent television documentary series, *Eyes on the Prize*, has done more to raise awareness of the civil rights movement, at least among the relatively few viewers who watch public television.

In the positive story of the sixties, both the civil rights movement and the New Left tried to bring about a more participatory democracy that would include the excluded: blacks, the poor, women. Political theorist and journalist James Miller organized his well-received history of the New Left, *Democracy Is in the Streets: From Port Huron to the Siege of Chicago*, around the slogan, participatory democracy. Significantly, Miller, like others generally sympathetic to the sixties, is ambivalent about this central idea. His book's subtitle expresses a downward trajectory: from Port Huron in 1962, where the idealistic young founders of SDS first issued the call for participatory democracy, to Chicago in 1968, where Mayor Richard Daley's police attacked antiwar protestors in front of the Democratic National Party Convention, provoking a televised riot that helped to polarize the country.

By the end of *Democracy Is in the Streets*, Miller's hopeful assertion that "the political vision of the New Left, and some its original spirit, have survived" carries less force than his somber history of a movement that betrayed the promise of Port Huron.[20] During the Siege of Chicago, "democracy in the streets" was redefined as participation in a riot. No wonder Miller sees the sixties as "A Collective Dream," the title of his last chapter, from which we have done well to awaken.

Unlike the negative cautionary tale, the positive inspirational story has a difficult time accounting for the end of the sixties, for the rejection, during the decades that followed, of participatory politics. The positive memory often turns out to be surprisingly fatalistic and negative, telling the story of the defeat of the "good" by the "bad" sixties." The image of Martin Luther King is supplanted by that of Malcolm X. The memory of nonviolent civil rights marchers is erased by the spectre of armed Black Panthers. The Port Huron convention becomes a hazy backdrop to the scenes of rioting in Chicago.

The positive sixties-as-metaphor is much more contested than the dominant, negative metaphor. There are at least three distinctive but overlapping stories of the struggle between the "good" and "bad" sixties; moreover, the storytellers disagree over which side is "good" and which is "bad."

The "organization versus movement" story focuses on the question of whether the civil rights movement and the New Left had too much or too little internal structure. In the more familiar version of this story,

SNCC and SDS began promisingly during the early sixties, but failed to transform their movements into strong, effective political organizations. Todd Gitlin, for example, describes himself as "one of those old New Leftists, anathema to all factions, who was broken up by the movement's whirling destruction and self-destruction as much as I had been inspired—even formed—by its birth."[21] The subtitle of Gitlin's popular history/memoir, *The Sixties*, effectively conveys his estimation of the early and late sixties: *Years of Hope, Days of Rage.*

In the competing version of this story, the mass movements that flowered after 1968, especially the antiwar, Black Power, and early women's liberation movements, represented radically new forms of organization, which were crushed by sectarianism from within and repression from without. According to Breines, who was the first to point out the distinction between the organization and the movement perspectives, "what was new about the New Left" was precisely its refusal to build a traditional, hierarchical organization.[22]

The story of the struggle between strategic and prefigurative politics, which overlaps with the organization versus movement tale, answers the question: what is the best way to make radical political change? The more typical version assumes that participatory democracy can not be implemented in any meaningful sense until the political system has been overhauled. During the sixties, the activists should have thought strategically, by concentrating on building an effective organization to lead the struggle for the complete restructuring of the government as quickly as possible. Instead, the movements after 1968 sabotaged their own cause by substituting narcissistic experimentation for political engagement.

In the alternate version of this tale, the later movements were positive examples of what Breines has called "prefigurative politics," the effort of activists to practice here and now the more participatory democracy which is their goal.[23] The advocates of greater organization were wrong to try to separate the means from the ends. By modeling participatory democracy, the radicals could have inspired others to imitate them, eventually building a movement capable of transforming all of society. Instead, the strategists sold out the revolution, settling for cosmetic reform which actually helped to prop up the corrupt system.

The "politics versus culture" story, which overlaps with both of the previous ones, is about two competing definitions of the political. In the more familiar version of this tale, politics is about power, specifically the question of who controls the government. A strategic and organizational approach could have enabled the New Left and the civil rights movement to make a lasting impact on the American political system.

Unfortunately, during the late sixties, the counterculture seemed to offer potential political activists the chance to rebel through music, drugs, clothing, hair, and "free love." In the view of historian David Farber, the counterculture "exchanged the political practice of people working together for social change for a fantasy of a mass youth culture already primed for revolution and just awaiting a TV commercial to tell them to go about their bloody business."[24]

In the less well known variation of the story, the turn toward culture represented not a rejection but an extension of politics to all areas of society where power is exercised. According to historian and activist Barbara Epstein, for example, the sixties movements took the first imperfect steps toward a "politics of cultural revolution," which could transform relations between men and women, and between people and their environment.[25]

Here, as in all three of the most popular versions of the good versus the bad sixties, the positive sixties-as-metaphor comes close to its negative counterpart. As we have seen, the critics of the sixties are also bitter toward the counterculture. The difference is that the critics reject *both* the politics and the culture of the sixties; in fact, they see almost no difference between the New Leftists and the hippies.

No matter which story predominates, the "bad"

sixties nearly always wins. Even the most nostalgic former activists admit that the sixties are over. The democratic movements were doomed to fail, and are unlikely to be reborn. As Gitlin says, "the upsurge was made from the living elements of a unique, unrepeatable history, under the spreading wings of the zeitgeist."[26]

A few storytellers never lose their tone of optimism, but their accounts are accordingly less compelling. For instance, Stewart Burns's brief history, *Social Movements of the 1960s: Searching for Democracy*, is permeated by an air of unconvincing cheeriness, from his descriptions of key figures (Rosa Parks "felt no fear") to his analysis of the tensions within the movements (the tendencies toward hierarchy and leaderlessness "complemented, connected and reinforced each other, and increasingly converged"). From the chapter titles, the reader would have little sense that the search for democracy was never completed ("We Shall All Be Free," "Everything is Possible," "Sisterhood is Powerful," "Bearing Fruit," "Readiness is All").[27]

The much more typical sympathetic stories of the sixties lead inexorably to the unhappy ending, as in Tom Hayden's conclusion that the "sixties movements were...blocked in the quest by the intervention of fate."[28] In many accounts, the movements seem to succumb to a fatal flaw, though its characterization varies. Mary King is a white, former SNCC organizer and the author of a thoughtful memoir of the civil rights movement that has received much less attention than those of her male contemporaries remembering the New Left. In her view, the internal diversity that made the early SNCC so successful also made failure inevitable: "if...the diversity of race, class, background, and experience of the staff members...was a key weakness that ultimately helped to destroy the group, it was also, ironically, our greatest strength."[29]

Often, the positive sixties-as-metaphor focuses on an image or event which symbolizes the tragic destiny that awaited the democratic movements. For instance, Kirkpatrick Sale, author of the first serious history of SDS, begins with the bomb accident which killed three members of Cathy Wilkerson's terrorist cell: "The explosion on West Eleventh Street was the ultimate symbol of SDS's tragic and ominous demise, and of the decade which had shaped it: a decade perhaps as fateful as any the nation has experienced...."[30] However, the most frequently used negative symbol is Chicago 1968, when antiwar protestors clashed with police outside the Democratic National Convention. David Farber, who has written the most complete history of those events echoes Mary King's view that the strengths of the movement were also its weaknesses:

> Chicago '68 was plagued with the problems that would
> eventually finish off the 1960s-style movement for social
> change. But without most of these problems—naivete,
> alienation, anti-intellectualism, stubborness, extreme
> moralism, youthful ignorance—there would not have been a
> movement in the first place.[31]

In light of such problems, it would seem to follow
that the failure of the sixties movements was probably
for the best. However, most tellers of the sympathetic
tale resist this conclusion, lending a kind of imbalance
to their stories. As with Gitlin, the days of rage
overshadow the years of hope. If the sixties have
anything to teach us, it can only be a lesson in what
not to do. For instance, an article on today's
environmental movement is subtitled, "Students say
they've learned from the mistakes of 6os strategies."[32]

The popular antifeminist Camille Paglia, who
considers herself a defender of the sixties, illustrates
how negative the "positive" memory of the sixties can
be. Paglia is as hostile as Roger Kimball (author of
Tenured Radicals) to the "academic leftists" who have
allegedly taken over higher education. But she disputes
his claim that they were politically active during the
sixties. The true radicals never made it through
graduate school, so the real problem in the academy is
"not a continuation of the 6os revolution, but an
evasion of it." Yet Paglia's "defense" of the sixties is
harsher than many a second thoughter's indictment:

> Everyone of my generation who preached free love is responsible for AIDS. The 60s revolution collapsed because of its own excesses. It followed and fulfilled its own inner historical pattern, a fall from Romanticism to Decadence.

If this is so, why should we cheer Paglia's conclusion that "sixties people were defeated, but we wised up and we're returning"?[33]

As with the negative sixties-as-metaphor, the positive one rests ultimately on an analogy between the history of the movement and the life cycle of the individual. Like young people everywhere, almost all the sixties activists have learned to put away their childish dreams and to accept the responsibilities of maturity. For instance, Miller concludes that the subsequent careers of the SDS founders show that "many veterans of the Movement have continued to apply the precepts of Port Huron in the light of their mature experience, evincing modesty in their immediate goals, pragmatism in their tactics, and a hard-earned realism in their evaluation of the prospects for social change."[34]

The sixties are, at best, something to be outgrown. Sooner or later, all the rebellious children come home. For example, the title of Hayden's memoir, *Reunion*, refers not only to a recent gathering of former SDS members, but to Hayden's personal situation: he is finally part of a happy family, and has reconciled with the father who disapproved of his radicalism in the past.[35] Now a California state legislator, Hayden is working within the conventional definition of democracy, rather than seeking to transform it.

This conflation of the personal and the political family, which appears frequently in both the negative and positive sixties-as-metaphors, helps to account for the national fascination with sixties fugitives from justice who resurface from the "underground" in order to turn themselves in. The repentance of older "young revolutionaries," most recently, Katherine Anne Power, confirms the truth of the negative interpretation of the sixties in a way that promises to reunite both the individual and the national families.

Power returned to stand trial as the driver of the get-away car in a politically-motivated bank robbery that led unexpectedly to the murder of Walter Schroeder, a Boston Catholic policeman. In explaining her decision to come back, Power emphasized her depression over being separated for so long from her parents and relatives. Although her lengthy prison sentence will keep her apart from her new husband and son for years, Power affirmed her commitment to rejoining both her families: "This time I am going to come back—not like the other times, when I've walked away from my family and everyone that I knew in my life. Now I have said I will not leave anymore."[36]

Significantly, the media covered the trial as a family

drama pitting the Powers family against the Schroeder family. Reporters ignored or ridiculed Power's half-hearted defense of her sixties ideals, while praising the testimony of Claire Schroeder, the murdered man's elder daughter, now a police sergeant herself. As spectators, the members of the national family experienced the satisfaction of simultaneously passing judgment on, and showing mercy toward, the latest sixties prodigal child, who will be allowed to return home after paying her debt to the injured family and to society.

"Sundered by a Memory"

But if the sixties generation has come home, why does the decade reappear so frequently in contemporary debates, and why is its meaning still contested? The sixties remain contested because the nineties are contested; the divisive issues of race and inequality that gave rise to the sixties movements are still with us. The political discourse surrounding the 1991 Gulf War, the 1992 Los Angeles riots, and the 1994 deaths of Richard Nixon and Jacqueline Kennedy Onassis reveal both the power of the negative story of the sixties in foreign and domestic policy, and the constant threat that the nation will again be divided over past and present.

In 1991, three years before President Clinton proclaimed that "the nation is one," while lifting the American embargo against Vietnam, his predecessor

George Bush announced that *he* had relegated the Vietnam War to the national memory. In Bush's Inaugural Address, he warned that "the final lesson of Vietnam is that no great nation can long afford to be sundered by a memory."[37] By the end of the 1991 Gulf War, he was convinced that the lesson had been learned. The defeat of Iraq had reunited the nation; Bush told a cheering audience that "we've kicked the Vietnam syndrome once and for all."[38] Perhaps, Clinton's position that *he* made the nation "one" is simply a partisan attempt at claiming credit.

Even before the U.S. victory in the Gulf War, the country had largely accepted the negative story of political protest. The nineties demonstrators themselves felt compelled to apologize for their sixties predecessors. A newspaper article on the opposition of members of the "Vietnam generation" to the impending Gulf War, reported that

> The primary legacy of the last war seems to be a sensitivity to the troops in the Gulf and a concern that any protest at home could leave them feeling scorned.... And virtually all the Vietnam protestors spoke with a tone of contrition about the unintended wounds they inflicted on the young men who served.[39]

Once the Gulf War broke out, the media largely ignored the antiwar demonstrators' attempts to distinguish themselves from their sixties forerunners, and focused instead on the very few who embraced the identification. For example:

> Saturday's demonstration in Washington was full of angry
> language about American imperialism and racism.
> There were mainstream peace groups and families with babies
> in strollers. But over all, the demonstration had the aura of the
> 60's, with shaggy youths pounding on tom-toms and numerous
> fringe groups like the Revolutionary Communist Youth Brigade
> with its chants of "Baghdad is everywhere; we are all Iraqis," or
> the Spartacist League with its banner reading "Defend Iraq!
> Defeat U.S. Imperialism."[40]

Such negative references to the sixties served to delegitimize the form as well as the content of opposition to the Gulf War. Beneath their camouflage of mainstream peace groups and babies in strollers, the protestors were revealed to be not democrats, but deviants. The Gulf War victory thus seemed to confirm the victory of the negative sixties-as-metaphor. The nation had been reunited, in the face of the threat from our enemies at home and abroad. Participatory politics was again shown to be childish and un-American.

However, the reunification was temporary. The Gulf War had merely masked the growing divisions among Americans between those who have homes, jobs, health insurance, access to good schools, or, at minimum, the right skin color, and those who do not. The commemorations of the war's first anniversary were strikingly pessimistic; a typical newspaper headline was "A Year After Victory, Joy is a Ghost."[41] So, perhaps, Clinton does deserve the credit for "finally" relegating the sixties to the national memory.

Or, is there something about the sixties that refuses to stay safely buried and forgotten? Even the *New York Times* can't make up its mind about whether the Vietnam War has or has not been relegated to the national memory. On November 11, 1992, an article on the tenth anniversary of the Vietnam Veterans Memorial reported that "The Wall has helped heal a nation. And the healing continues."[42] But, a little over six months later, when veterans booed Clinton's Memorial Day speech at the Wall, a front page story acknowledged that "despite his appeal for reconciliation, Vietnam remained a national wound that will not heal."[43]

Why have recent Presidents been so eager to slam the door on the decade? For Bush, like his predecessor Ronald Reagan, the answer seems obvious. Conservatives would naturally be expected to want to bury all traces of the political movements and social changes which they opposed, then and now. But then why, despite the national turn toward conservatism in recent decades, do its leading voices so frequently call our attention to the memory they want to erase?

The Clinton case is more complicated. As a Vietnam War protestor himself, the President presumably believes that the sixties movements had some value. But in a more conservative era, his antiwar activism, and especially his avoidance of the draft, have become political liabilities.[44] So, for Clinton, what must be forgotten is not merely that the country was divided, but that he was on the wrong side of the divide.

Yet, Clinton patently feels that some aspects of the sixties *should* be remembered, or he wouldn't try so hard to identify himself with President Kennedy. Clinton's 1992 Presidential campaign featured the image of teenage Bill shaking hands with John Kennedy during the sixties. Yet, a few months after Clinton's remarks on the embargo, he delivered the eulogy at the funeral of Richard Nixon, Kennedy's opponent in 1960, and the President whose decisions to expand the Vietnam War twenty-something Bill had protested. Why wasn't this perceived as blatant political opportunism? Or, are Clinton's actions less inconsistent than they appear to be?

The American desire to forget the divisions of the sixties is bound up with the desire to remember and reenact a mythical moment of national unity, such as the optimistic "Camelot" era symbolized by the Kennedys. For example, in a column on the funeral of Jacqueline Kennedy Onassis, President Kennedy's widow, *New York Times* columnist Frank Rich claims that "her death brought Americans together as nothing else has lately, resurrecting a shared memory of the national idealism thought to have been buried forever in the cynical decades since Dallas."[45] However, another journalist counters that the sense of togetherness is illusory, that, in fact, Jackie's "passing broke a link to a time when politicians were often heroes, a time of sweet optimism that was soured by Vietnam and Watergate."[46] Both articles suggest that the time of sweet optimism was brief, followed by decades of cynicism.

Then and now, the mythical moment of national unity demands little of ordinary Americans, certainly not their participation in political decision-making. The role of the citizen is chiefly that of the spectator, preferably idealistic and optimistic, who cheers on the actors at center stage. At most, citizens are called to play supporting roles as taxpayers, soldiers, and so on. The celebration of the thirtieth anniversary of the first landing of human beings on the moon illustrates the gap between the mere sensation of collective bonding, and the concrete experience of participating with others in a common project. A reporter observed that

> Conversations with dozens of Americans find a pensive, even melancholy longing for the heady days of July 1969, when the nation, despite crippling divisions over issues like the Vietnam War and racial equality, somehow still managed to pull together and collectively focus on and attain an awesome goal. Today, many Americans say, that special measure of togetherness has been lost while the divisions remain.[47]

But what did Americans, other than the astronauts and space center personnel, actually *do* to pull together and attain the goal? They "collectively focused" on television. No wonder such a passive kind of "togetherness" can not overcome real political divisions over race and war. Remembering the moon landing or Camelot as a moment of national unity also requires forgetting how divided the nation really was over the Vietnam War, civil rights, and John Kennedy himself.

Richard Nixon's surprising reemergence as a respected elder statesman in the decade before his death in 1994 also indicates a national desire for reconciliation at the price of forgetfulness. Although he was the only President to have resigned in disgrace, Nixon's stock has gone up as the value of the sixties has gone down. Perhaps he looks better because what he opposed—protest, anarchy, a generation run amok— looks worse. In the case of both Nixon and Onassis, the climax of national togetherness occurred at a state funeral, during which any lingering, negative memories were symbolically buried. "Nixon Funeral Becomes A Rite of Reconciliation," declared the *New York Times*, attributing the presence of President Clinton and other dignitaries to "a national readiness to let bygones be bygones."[48]

Both Clinton and Bush want to use the selective national memory of the sixties to make a point about contemporary politics. They are able to do so only because our collective memory of the sixties is grounded in the national memory of previous democratic moments in American history, such as the sit-down strikes of the 1930s and the Populist farmers' movement at the end of the nineteenth century. Both Presidents hope to remind us of past divisions in order to reunite us in the present, but on the basis of a mythical past, not a shared public life.

However, it is not memory which divides us. The nation is not "one" for many of the same reasons that inspired the democratic movements of the sixties, including inequality and injustice. Americans have been unable to agree on the meaning of the sixties, because they cannot agree on the meaning of the nineties. But by discouraging participatory politics, our national memory of the sixties makes it harder to engage the difficult issues that divide us today.

Shortly after the Gulf War, a corporate executive took out a full-page advertisement in the *New York Times* calling for the use of military methods to solve civilian problems, and to bring Americans together. "Operation Recovery," the ad read, would be led by the hero of the war:

> ...General Norman Schwarzkopf. A man who understands objectives, strategies, and tactics. One who has proven that he can lead an assault and rally forces to victory. Serving in a civilian capacity, he would enlist the aid of captains of industry. More importantly, I am certain the American people would get behind it.

> Operation Desert Storm was masterfully executed. I truly
> believe that Operation Recovery will lead to a victory on the
> home front.[49]

Shortly after this ad appeared, the Los Angeles riots of 1992 reminded the nation how close we were to defeat on the home front. As in the debate over the Gulf War, conservatives blamed the present crisis on the sixties. One week after the rioting triggered by the not-guilty verdict in the trial of four Los Angeles police officers for the beating of Rodney King, White House press secretary Marlin Fitzwater announced the Bush administration's position on the underlying causes: "We believe that many of the root problems that have resulted in inner-city difficulties were started in the 60's and 70's, and that they have failed."[50] The literal meaning of this statement was unclear: how can *problems* fail?

However, Fitzwater indicated elsewhere that he was referring to the social welfare *programs* of the Great Society era. And his choice of words may have been deliberate; the effect of using the word "problems" in place of the similar-sounding "programs" is to suggest that the programs *were* the problems. According to a reporter, Bush's supporters blamed the riots on "an attitude that they say prevailed during the sixties, with Democratic encouragement, that poor people were not responsible for their behavior."[51]

Two weeks later, Vice President Dan Quayle

embraced this latest variation of sixties-bashing. Including himself as a member, Quayle zeroed in on

> one unfortunate legacy of the baby boomer generation. When we were young, it was fashionable to declare war against traditional values. Indulgence and self-gratification seemed to have no consequences. Many of our generation glamorized casual sex and drug use, evaded responsibility and trashed authority.
>
> Today the boomers are middle-aged and middle class. The responsibility of having families has helped many recover traditional values. And, of course, the great majority of those in the middle class survived the turbulent legacy of the 60's and 70's. But many of the poor, with less to fall back on, did not.[52]

The controversy over Quayle's chief example of the decline of traditional values, the television character Murphy Brown's decision to become a single mother, overshadowed the new twist that had been given to the negative sixties-as-metaphor. Instead of taking aim at the middle-class rebels who largely composed the New Left, Quayle zeroes in on the people whom they were trying to help. Unlike the great majority of the middle class, who transcended the legacy of the sixties by maturing into responsible heads of families, the poor, especially blacks, continue to glamorize sex and drugs, evade responsibility, and trash authority. Present-day liberals, particularly those in the Democratic party, are still to blame for their continued endorsement of failed welfare policies and affirmative action, but basically, it is the poor who have failed themselves. The chorus of assent drowned out the few alternative voices trying to argue that the riots revealed not the failure of the sixties movements, but the persistence of the racial and economic inequalities against which they fought.

In the nineties, the War on Poverty has become the War on the Poor. Army troops were sent to Los Angeles to restore order. Although these units were not originally intended for riot control, their commander explained that "in constrained and urban terrain, and in situations where you need lots of soldier power deployed very rapidly to deal with a crisis situation, the light forces have great utility."[53] The general in charge of the operation admitted that "it's depressing that we have a situation in America that's brought us here." But, he adds that "we know that we have trained, ready, compassionate, and very sensitive soldiers, and we are going to regain the safe environment that our civilians want."[54] Whether the problem is a domestic riot or a foreign war, there is a military solution available. Operation Desert Storm has literally become Operation Recovery.

In the aftermath of Los Angeles, the civil rights movement of the nineties no longer tries to organize a democratic mass movement. Shortly after the riots, former SNCC leader John Lewis, now a Congressman from Georgia, explained the difference between the sixties and the nineties. In an article headlined "The

Civil Rights Battle Was Easy Next to the Problems of the Ghetto," Lewis explained that it "was easier to go and sit at a lunch counter all day and let a lighted cigarette get put out in your hair…. It was easier to march across the bridge in Selma and get tear-gassed." If today's problems are so intractable, then all the left can do, according to the reporter, is "dream of a new Dr. King."[55]

Since the sixties, both the left and the right have moved away from participatory politics, the right because mass political action has always been unnecessary and threatening, the left because the enduring lesson of the end of the sixties is that such action is at best futile and at worst dangerous. Although the positive story of the sixties tells of democracy while the negative story tells of totalitarianism or chaos, both versions tend to discourage participatory politics today.

Comparing these stories of the sixties to the brief histories of SNCC and SDS in the previous chapter suggests that neither the positive nor the negative memory is completely true or false. SNCC and SDS did realize participatory democracy, if only for brief moments. The vision of shared political and economic power came to life during the early years of SNCC, when rural black Southerners were inspired to "stand" themselves, as well as during the few times when ERAP helped poor urban Northerners to build vibrant community organizations. The positive stories of the sixties remind us of these democratic moments, without offering much hope for their revival. The negative stories magnify the very real problems of self-indulgence, separatism, and so on, while obscuring or disparaging the very real, historically significant achievements of participatory politics, including the end of legal segregation and of the Vietnam War. Because the negative version dominates the national memory, the full story of the participation of thousands of ordinary Americans in the struggle for democracy is unknown to most of us, even to the activists who carry on that struggle today.

Cesar Chavez addressing a rally in Santa Maria, California in October, 1972. (Archives of Labor and Urban Affairs, Wayne State University)

"This American Democracy": Whites pour sugar, ketchup, and mustard on lunch counter sit-in demonstrators, Jackson, Mississippi, 1963. (AP/Wide World photos)

Resting during the March on Washington led by
Dr. Martin Luther King, Jr., August 28, 1963. (Courtesy
of the Library of Congress, Prints and Photographs division)

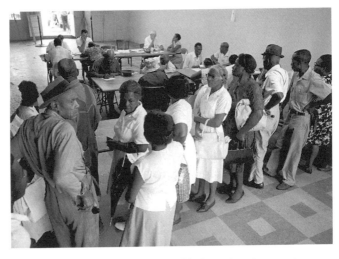

Participatory democracy: Southern blacks registering to vote for the first time. (Courtesy of the Library of Congress, Prints and Photographs division)

The politics of confrontation during the late sixties. (UPI/Bettmann)

Participatory politics today: Chester,
Pennsylvania residents protest against an
incinerator located in their neighborhood, in
April 1993. (Delaware County *Daily Times,* 4/21/94)

FOUR

"IS THIS AMERICA?"

IN her speech to the Democratic National Party Convention in 1964, SNCC organizer Fannie Lou Hamer claimed a place for the civil rights struggle at the very heart of American history:

> Is this America? The land of the free and the home of the brave?

> Where we have to sleep with our telephones off the hook,
> because our lives be threatened daily?[1]

Hamer was referring to her own experiences as a Southern black, of being fired, arrested, and beaten for simply trying to register to vote. The decision on whether to seat the insurgent MFDP delegation was really a decision on the identity of America. What would the answer to her question be: the land of the free, or the land of the slaves?

Hamer's questions are still relevant thirty years later. The answer is that, thoughout its history, America has been both. There are two American democratic traditions: the dominant one, in which meaningful political participation has been limited to the few, but also a mostly hidden one in which Americans have struggled for and practiced a more participatory democracy. Fannie Lou Hamer had activist predecessors, although she was probably unaware of them, just as most Americans are unfamiliar with her today.

The story we tell ourselves about the sixties is a chapter of the story we tell ourselves about America. The sixties have become a metaphor for a more participatory democracy, because the image of America has stood for democracy throughout its history. Both the negative and positive stories of the sixties recapitulate the memories of earlier democratic moments in American history. The dominant narrative has taught that participatory democracy is un-American, although fainter voices have kept alive the memory and promise of what Hamer called the "true" democracy.

The Government versus the Spirit of the People

Like the stories we tell ourselves about American history, the meaning of democracy has been and continues to be contested.

Nowadays, it has been largely forgotten that there was a genuine struggle between two definitions of democracy at the nation's founding.[2] The losing side, known today only as the Anti-Federalists, are dimly remembered for what they opposed, not for what they advocated.[3] In fact, the Federalists who wrote the Constitution were the radicals, while their opponents expressed a classical theory of direct democracy that corresponded more closely to American political practice at the time.

James Madison and Alexander Hamilton explained the new political theory in the *Federalist Papers*, which they wrote, along with John Jay, during the fight over the ratification of the proposed Constitution. Their starting point, surprising in the wake of the War for Independence, was that human beings cannot be trusted to govern themselves. As Madison put it, in a famous passage from "Federalist #51":

> But what is government itself but the greatest of all reflections on human nature? If men were angels, no government would

be necessary. If angels were to govern men, neither external nor internal controls on government would be necessary. In framing a government which is to be administered by men over men, the great difficulty is this: you must first enable the government to control the governed; and in the next place, you must oblige it to control itself.[4]

Angels could make a go of participatory democracy, but men must not be allowed to rule themselves. How can the government control both the people and itself? The Federalists proposed three constitutional safeguards, which became the defining features of American democracy: representation, separation of powers, and size. Direct participation would be limited to the election of superior men, supposedly to represent, but actually to control their inferiors. In fact, most Americans would not even have the right to vote for their so-called representatives. The President was to be chosen by the Electoral College, and the Senators by the state legislatures. Although the members of the House of Representatives were to be elected directly, only white men with property could vote. African Americans were accorded the dubious honor of being counted as three-fifths of a vote for the purpose of calculating the number of representatives to which Southern states would be entitled.

Since even the most superior of men were inferior to angels, they too must be controlled while in office. In Madison's well-known phrase, "Ambition must be made to counteract ambition."[5] The key was the separation of powers; each of the three branches of the national government would need the cooperation of at least one other in order to act, while the division between the national federal government and the states would further inhibit officials from abusing their powers.[6]

The Federalists' most innovative suggestion was that a nation should be large. In #10, Madison argued that the smaller the country, the greater its vulnerability to disruptions by minorities, or even majorities of citizens united against the common good. The best method of "curing the mischiefs of faction" was to increase the size of the nation:

> Extend the sphere and you take in a great variety of parties and interests; you make it less probable that a majority of the whole will have a common motive to invade the rights of other citizens; or if such a common motive exists, it will be more difficult for all who feel it to discover their own strength and to act in unison with each other.[7]

But if a large republic would prevent majorities from coming together to do anything bad, it would also prevent them from uniting to do anything good. The governmental gridlock so frequently complained of today is the logical result of a Constitution designed to resist majority initiatives and to favor the status quo. The paradox of American democracy has been neatly captured in the observation by J.G.A. Pocock, the noted authority on the origins of the Anglo-American political tradition, that "all government was the people's, and yet the people never directly governed."[8]

The Federalists' writings suggest that the new democratic theory was intended, at least in part, to preclude action by the majority, who had little or no wealth, against the minority including most of the Federalists, who were better off.[9] In #10, Madison states bluntly that "those who hold and those who are without property have ever formed distinct interests in society." The Revolutionary War had unleashed the poor, who had done most of the fighting, and who clamored for abolishing the debts they had incurred by being away from their farms and shops. Certainly, Madison had the recent Shay's Rebellion in mind when he offered examples of the dangerous "common motives" which a large republic would prevent: "a rage for paper money, for an abolition of debts, for an equal division of property, or for any other improper or wicked project."[10]

The Anti-Federalists were not defenders of the propertyless, who had no voice in the debate over the Constitution. But the opponents of ratification did favor the more direct democracy that was currently practiced in town meetings and state legislatures, although they agreed that the franchise should continue to be limited to white propertied men. Their experience of democracy led them to reject nearly every Federalist assumption: that human nature is purely ambitious and inalterable, that representation is preferable to participation; that separation of powers is desirable; and that a large nation is better than a small one.

From the Anti-Federalist perspective, a government designed to control men rather than to improve them was doomed to fail:

> Government operates upon the spirit of the people, as well as the spirit of the people operates upon it—and if they are not comformable to each other, the one or the other will prevail.... Our duty is to frame a government friendly to liberty and the rights of mankind, which will tend to cherish and cultivate a love of liberty among our citizens.[11]

The suggestion that government should cherish and cultivate certain attitudes is likely to seem peculiar and even threatening to the citizens of the nineties who have inherited the Federalists' views. Similarly, the Anti-Federalists' fears for the future, should the Constitution be ratified, are apt to sound hysterical or paranoid:

> It is next to impossible to enslave a people immediately after a firm struggle against oppression, while the sense of past injury is recent and strong. But after some time this impression naturally wears off; the ardent glow of freedom gradually evaporates.... Such declension in all those vigorous springs of action necessarily produces a supineness. The altar of liberty is no longer watched with such attentive assiduity...and, if the nation happens to enjoy a series of prosperity, voluptuousness, excessive fondness for riches, and luxury gain admission and establish themselves—these produce venality and corruption of

every kind, which open a fatal avenue to bribery. Hence it follows, that in the midst of this general contagion a few men—or one—more powerful than all the others, industriously endeavor to obtain all authority; and by means of great wealth—or embezzling the public money, —perhaps totally subvert the government, and erect a system of aristocratical or monarchic tyranny in its room.[12]

The idea that an active citizenry is the best defense against tyranny seems dated to contemporary Americans, who have grown accustomed to their passive roles in the political system. Moreover, the Anti-Federalists' prediction that the American government would be replaced by aristocracy or monarchy has not literally come true. In fact, most of the least democratic features of the original government, such as the denial of voting rights to women, people of color, and the poor, have been gradually eliminated. But their prophecy of a nation weakened by "prosperity... excessive fondness for riches... venality and corruption" has been at least partly realized. So, too, has been their prediction of a decline in the "springs" of political action, the town meetings and other local venues for popular participation. In the words of the political theorist Hannah Arendt, "in this republic...there was no space reserved, no room left for the exercise of precisely those qualities which had been instrumental in building it."[13]

Ironically, the Federalists' triumph confirms the Anti-Federalists' insight into the mutual relationship between the government and the spirit of the people. Despite his theory that human nature is immutable, Madison's political practice was close to his opponents view that the government must "cherish and cultivate" the correct attitudes in its citizens. The Federalists fully expected that their new political institutions would inculcate the new theory of democracy in succeeding generations. Their success is evidenced by the fact that their descendants are barely aware of the other side of the argument.[14]

Less than fifty years after the ratification of the Constitution, the French visitor Alexis Tocqueville provided eyewitness testimony on the state of the relationship between the new government and the spirit of the people. At first, Tocqueville was excited about the participatory politics which he saw, or thought he saw, in the town meetings of New England, and the associations that proliferated during the Jacksonian era. The United States seemed to have reconciled the two major trends of the age of democracy: equality and liberty, by which Tocqueville meant participation in public affairs. The town meetings and associations were schools of democracy, which taught Americans about participatory politics by giving them opportunities to practice it, in both senses of the word, as part of their everyday lives.

For all his enthusiasm about the United States, however, Tocqueville also noted the persistence of inequality, particularly the forced removal of the Indians from the land coveted by white settlers, and the continued enslavement of the blacks.[15]

By the time he came to write the second volume of his classic, *Democracy in America*, Tocqueville had become more pessimistic. Like the Anti-Federalists, he observed that the love of freedom was losing ground to the love of riches, opening the door to tyranny. However, he anticipated something new, not the aristocracy or monarchy feared by the Anti-Federalists, but what he called "democratic despotism":

> I see an innumerable multitude of men, alike and equal, constantly circling around in pursuit of the petty and banal pleasures with which they glut their souls. Each one of them, withdrawn into himself, is almost unaware of the fate of the rest.... Over this kind of men stands an immense, protective power which is alone responsible for securing their enjoyment and watching over their fate. That power is absolute, thoughtful of detail, orderly, provident, and gentle. It would resemble parental authority if, father-like, it tried to prepare its charges for a man's life, but on the contrary, it only tries to keep them in perpetual childhood.... It is not at all tyrannical, but it hinders, restrains, enervates, stifles, and stultifies so much that in the end each nation is no more than a flock of timid and hardworking animals with the government as its shepherd.[16]

By the 1830s, the new American political system had already begun to educate the people in a new spirit.

Tocqueville foresaw a government that was not tyrannical, but overly solicitous, taking "fatherly" care of its citizens, but keeping them in perpetual childhood. Treated as children, the people were becoming timid and docile, preoccupied with pursuing material possessions, and content to give over responsibility for taking care of themselves. Tocqueville saw just one remedy: democratic participation in local politics.

> Citizens who are bound to take part in public affairs must turn from their private interests and occasionally take a look at something other than themselves .... Local liberties, then, which induce a great number of citizens to value the affection of their kindred and neighbors, bring men constantly into contact, despite the instincts which separate them, and force them to help one another.[17]

Today, near the end of the twentieth century, many of Tocqueville's predictions have come true. Most Americans have become more alike in putting private ahead of public affairs, sheep-like on the rare occasions when they participate in politics. However, Tocqueville would be suprised by the vast economic, social, and political inequalities that remain. And while the power of the government over its citizens has increased dramatically, as he anticipated, neither he nor the citizens of today would probably describe it as "thoughtful of detail, orderly, provident, and gentle." Tocqueville would also be deeply troubled by the intrusion of the global economy into national and even local politics. Dwarfed by the huge political and economic organizations that dominate their lives, contemporary citizens have fewer and fewer opportunities to participate democratically. If anything were to give Tocqueville hope, it would be the fact that participatory democracy remains alive, but in scattered neighborhoods and workplaces, rarely in the halls of government.

Democratic Moments

Throughout American history, participatory democracy has reappeared. During their long struggles for democracy, blacks, women, factory workers, farmers, and many others created what Sara Evans and Harry Boyte, who have tried to popularize the hidden history and practice of participation in America, have called "free spaces." These are usually small-scale settings, such as community organizations, local unions, cooperatives, advocacy groups, independent parties or caucuses of major parties, where people learn about democratic participation through participating.[18] At key moments in this nation's past, free spaces have grown into full-fledged movements that promised to transform the entire political system.

A few of the movement leaders have been accorded minor places in the pantheon of American history, such as Frederick Douglass, who is remembered more for the fact that this former slave shook hands with President Lincoln, than for his eloquent attacks on a democratic system that treated blacks as second class citizens both before and after the Civil War. But there have been many more, anonymous Americans who have carried on the participatory tradition, often sacrificing all they had, up to and including their lives. They were the brave men and women, black and white, who broke the law to help slaves to freedom on the underground railroad; the young "girls" toiling in the textile mills of Lowell, Massachusetts, who went on strike more than once during the 1830s to protest wage cuts; the miners and their families who were shot or burned to death in the massacre that ended the fifteen-month strike in Ludlow, Colorado; the suffragettes who risked arrest for the right to vote during the late-nineteenth and early-twentieth centuries; the Socialists who spent years in prison for their refusal to be drafted into World War I, which they regarded as a conflict among kings, not ordinary people; and many, many others.[19]

The democratic movements with the greatest transformative potential in American history were the Populist movement of farmers during the 1880s and 1890s, the labor movement during the sit-down era of the 1930s, and the civil rights movement and the New Left of the 1960s.

In his definitive history of the American Populists,

Lawrence Goodwyn shows how Southern and Western farmers built a democratic movement that enabled them to take back control of the fruits of their own labor, and to mount an effective challenge to a political system dominated by centralized corporate and state power.[20] By the 1880s, the independent yeoman farmers that Thomas Jefferson described as the backbone of American democracy, had been forced into dependence on banks and credit merchants for the seeds and equipment necessary for planting and harvesting their crops, on middlemen for arranging their sale, and on railroads for transporting them.

The Populists built a democratic movement through a sequential process that began with the formation of an autonomous institution, the National Farmers' Alliance and Industrial Union, in which they experimented with alternatives to the credit system. This led to the development of the first large-scale workers' cooperative in history, which inspired millions of farmers to join the new movement and create their own cooperatives. These experiences, plus a network of 40,000 Alliance lecturers, helped the new recruits to understand the deeper issues behind their plight, especially the unequal distribution of political and economic power under capitalism. Once "educated," the members of the movement formed the People's Party, which came close to electing a President, William Jennings Bryan, in 1896, and to changing the face of twentieth-century American politics.

At its height, the Populist movement nearly succeeded in bridging the divisions among the American people that have thwarted democratic movements through this nation's history. Although its core constituency was white, Anglo-Saxon, Protestant farmers, the movement brought together two of three geographical regions, the South and the West, included blacks and women as members and leaders, and reached out to the urban, immigrant workers of the North.

Critical to the success of the movement was the development of a "movement culture," which helped the members to achieve both the "individual self-respect" and the "collective self-confidence" necessary for democracy. Through the experience of participation as interpreted and supported by the movement culture, the individual Populist gained what Martin Luther King described as a "sense of somebodiness,"[21] and the movement as a whole gained confidence in the power of collective action. Together, these enabled large numbers of people to make the transition from what Goodwyn calls "a mass folkway of resignation" to a "mass folkway of autonomy."[22]

But the spectacular rise of the Populist movement was followed quickly by an equally spectacular decline. Like other major American movements, the history of the Populists tends to confirm the conclusion of sociologist and former SDS leader Richard Flacks: "the U.S. left is unparalleled in the degree to which organizations came into being, experienced relatively brief periods of rising strength and impact, only to rapidly decline."[23] Racism and xenophobia hampered the Populists efforts to reach out to urban immigrants and to black sharecroppers. Also, the movement entered national politics before organizing a truly broad and committed base. Once it was embroiled in electoral campaigns, the People's Party became obsessed with a single issue, the question of the silver versus the gold standard, which was co-opted easily by one of the two mainstream parties, the Democrats. Meanwhile, with little attention being paid to the grassroots, the banks were able to destroy the cooperatives. Without a place to practice democracy in daily life, the members of the movement drifted away.

In Goodwyn's view, the tragedy of the Populist "moment" was that when the farmers' movement was ready to challenge the premises of capitalism and the corporate state, the labor movement was not.[24] By this time, American industrial workers had not created a mass movement and a movement culture. By the 1930s, many farmers had already been forced to migrate to the city, and the millions who still remained on the land had been reduced to tenantry and sharecropping. The years of dependence following the collapse of the

Populist movement had whittled away their hard-won political self-respect and collective self-confidence, which the urban workers finally acquired through the sit-down strikes.

Although factory workers had been organizing themselves since the beginning of the Industrial Revolution, American capitalists had successfully resisted the unionization of the vast majority, by taking advantage of the heterogeneity of the American workforce to "divide and conquer"; by blocking labor legislation, from bills against child labor to bills that would have legalized unions; and by using government troops and their own armed gangs to break the major strikes that miners, railroad workers, and many others took against terrible odds.

In the "Ludlow massacre," for instance, John D. Rockefeller smashed a fifteen-month strike by 9,000 coal miners, by authorizing the Colorado National Guard, which consisted mostly of professional gunmen and others on the payroll of the coal companies, to attack the tent colony where the miners and their families were camped. Women and children huddled in pits underneath their tents while a battle raged between the miners, who only had rifles, and the guardsmen, who used a machine gun mounted on a hill above the camp. The Guard also set off two bombs. After twelve hours, the officers ordered the militia to pour coal oil on the tents and set them ablaze. Women and children fled from the pits while the militia looted and killed at least three unarmed prisoners. The next day, in one pit, the miners discovered the bodies of two women and eleven children, suffocated or burned to death.[25]

Still, each small victory and even each defeat gave workers the experience of participation, and helped keep alive a movement culture. The Great Depression, which began in 1929, forced the issue of the chasm between the power and wealth of American industry and the powerlessness and vulnerability of the workers who had built it. Led by the militant Congress of Industrial Workers (CIO), the sit-down strikes began in Flint, Michigan, in late 1936, when over 110,000 autoworkers put down their tools at General Motors but stayed in the plants, making it impossible to bring in strikebreakers. After minor but bloody skirmishes outside the plants, which involved the women's auxiliary, who were responsible for getting food to the strikes, the crisis came when Governor Frank Murphy threatened to remove the strikers by force. After a tense meeting with the charismatic head of the CIO, John L. Lewis, Murphy decided to hold back the troops, and in February 1937, the company agreed to recognize the fledgling United Auto Workers union (UAW).[26]

Sit-down strikes spread across the country, bringing the movement experience and culture to hundreds of thousands of workers. In 1935, Congress passed the National Labor Relations Act (NLRB), which gave industrial workers the legal right to form unions. With an active, expanding grassroots base, it seemed that the labor movement would continue to grow to the point where it could challenge successfully the basic structures of both the economic and the political systems.

While union membership did rise during World War II and the post war years, the labor movement shifted away from organizing the unorganized to negotiating greater benefits for the workers already under contract. In doing so, the movement missed a potential opportunity to build the coalition between whites and African Americans that had eluded the Populists. During the McCarthy era, union leadership got rid of suspected Communists and other dissidents who might have pushed the labor movement to take more radical stances in favor of democracy.

Today, the labor movement has declined along with American industry, which has eliminated or transferred many jobs overseas. In the unstable global economy of the nineties, multinational corporations are largely unaccountable to national governments, let alone to the workers of a particular country. American unions, few of which are run democratically, now represent slightly over 10% of the workforce.[27]

These brief glimpses of the two most significant democratic movements prior to the sixties in the United States reveal that the New Left was not as "new" as its members claimed. The civil rights movement, too, was carrying on a vibrant tradition of participatory politics, including a history of collective resistance to racism that had begun almost as soon as the first Africans stepped off the slave ships, in chains.

The rise and fall of the two most participatory organizations of the sixties, SNCC and SDS, parallels the trajectories of the Populists and the sit-down strikers in several key respects. Both SNCC and SDS were strongest during their earliest days, when they focused on the creation of local community organizations in which Southern blacks and Northern poor whites learned about and practiced participatory politics as a way of solving their specific problems. Like the Populists, the sixties groups achieved important early victories, which propelled them on to the national scene before they had a chance to develop strong mass bases that could have better resisted repression and cooptation. Once SNCC and SDS had moved away from the democratic participation that had brought them success, they soon collapsed.

In fact, because of television's ability to flash pictures of a demonstration around the country within, at most, a few hours of the event, the ascent and decline of SNCC and SDS occurred much more rapidly than their predecessors'. This meant that the sixties organizers had less time to educate and test their members in the crucible of political practice.

Ironically, the comparative slowness of communications during the eras of the Populists and sit-down strikers may have enabled them to do the slow, hard work of political organizing and education.

Most of the ordinary Americans who participated in the sixties movements were unaware of the history that they were, to a large extent, reenacting. Some of the organizers did have direct ties to the earlier movements; in fact, a sizable proportion of the students who ratified The Port Huron Statement were "red diaper" babies, children of the "Old" Leftists who had played active roles in the labor struggles during the thirties.[28] But even they had to contend with the distorted versions of history that permeated American political culture, then and now.

The Populist movement itself is dimly remembered, if at all. William Jennings Bryan made a famous speech for (or against?) silver (or gold? who can keep it straight?), and his followers are recalled as racist "rednecks," who had to be dragged, kicking and screaming, into the twentieth century. Or they're confused with the Progressives, who seem to have had something to do with trying to clean up government around the turn of the century, or maybe that was some other group that started with a "P"?

The dominant story of labor during the thirties dismisses the most radical organizers, those who linked the battle for better working conditions to the fight for greater democracy, as Communist "agitators," and the workers who followed them, as mere "dupes." During the thirties, many leftists did join the Communist and Socialist parties, but, for decades, the label "Communist" (or "Socialist" or "Marxist-Leninist") was used generically to tar with the brush of "un-Americanism" any attempt to question the existing distribution of economic and political power. In the aftermath of the Cold War, "special interests" has become the disparaging term of choice for unions.

Ironically, Americans rarely identify themselves anymore as "workers," although nearly all of them work for wages (with the sizable exception of the unemployed, who wish they did), but instead feel a sense of kinship with farmers, of whom there are very few left. They teach their children to sing about Old Macdonald's farm (ee-i-ee-i-o), when in fact Old Mac has been sent off to a retirement "village," his son is a computer programmer with a few geraniums in front of his suburban "ranch" house, and the family farm is now a tiny parcel of the million acres owned by the "agribusiness" division of a multinational corporation. The people who actually harvest Old Mac's corn and take care of his pigs are migrant framworkers, mostly dark-skinned immigrants. What redblooded American would identify with "those people," who are probably all illegal, anyway?

Frontier Democracy

Just as the story of the sixties is contested, so is the story of American history as a whole. The dominant narratives of past democratic movements, including the Populists, the sit-down striker, the civil rights movement, and the New Left, recapitulate a paradigmatic American story that is fundamentally hostile to democratic participatory politics.

The idea that a story of American history dominates politics and political culture seems to fly in the face of the popular, and often scholarly, view that this nation is uniquely unconstrained by its parts. The American story is that there is no story. This is the nation of immigrants and refugees who came and keep coming, whether invited or not, precisely in order to escape confining traditions and identities. In the "New World," according to literacy historian R. W. B. Lewis, each of us is as innocent as an "American Adam...poised at the start of a new history."[29] Each Adam is free to write his own history, and to define his own place in it. The only story that we share is that each of us is the author and hero of his own story.

In the consensus interpretation of American history, this country is seen as "exceptional." Because Americans never had to overthrow a feudal system on their own territory, they avoided the deep social, economic, and political divisions that characterize European nations. Freed from constricting traditions and hierarchies, Americans had more opportunities to decide their own fate than any other people in history. Natural abundance and ethnic heterogeneity also helped to forestall class conflict, and to encourage upward mobility. The "absence of feudalism and the presence of the liberal idea," as influential historian Louis Hartz put it, allowed the theory of the self-made man to become reality.[30] The use of the noun "man" is more than simply old-fashioned, this is a masculine discourse in which a woman's role is to be either the helpmeet or the prize, or both.

In the words of Perry Miller, best known for his work on Puritanism, "an American identity is not something to be inherited so much as something to be achieved."[31] Unconstrained by history, memory, or community, the pioneer treks across the plains to claim his own piece of land; the orphan works hard and ends up owning the factory; the poor boy grows up to become President.

Self-made men are independent of each other and of government. Participatory politics is unnecessary and even dangerous, because the only reason for government is to keep men apart. The key political moment in this story is the drafting of a Constitution that would prevent Americans from interfering with each other's efforts to make a self in the only arena that really matters: the market.

The story of the self-made men complements but

also masks a darker and more complex narrative about those moments in which Americans *do* act together on the basis of shared tradition and membership. In this story, a national mission unites self-made individuals through violent action against people of color and other "aliens." The central political event in this version of American history is not the ratification of the Constitution, but the encounter with the wilderness and its inhabitants.

The Frontier Myth, as cultural historian Richard Slotkin has shown, adapts traditional heroic and religious epics to the project of civilizing a New World.[32] Far from being innocent Adams, the colonists brought their pasts with them.

The New England Puritans first articulated the themes of what came to be the dominant American narrative. As emigrants from the "Old" World to an already inhabited "new" one, they were unsure about their relationship to the society they had left, and to the wilderness they had entered. Looking east, across the Atlantic toward Europe, the members of the Massachusetts Bay Company believed that they were carrying out a religious "errand into the wilderness" on behalf of those who remained behind.[33] In the words of Governor John Winthrop, they saw themselves as a "city on a hill," a religious model for all nations.[34]

Facing west, toward the wilderness, the new Americans confronted the urgent task of survival in what they viewed as a hostile wasteland, inhabited by barely human people whom they called "savages." As the colonists gained confidence and ventured farther into this wilderness, they were suprised to find themselves attracted to, as well as repulsed by, the abundant natural world and by the freedom of the "Indian" way of life. At the same time, the Americans came to resent European indifference and condescension, even as prosperity made the errand seem less urgent, especially to the next generation.

The Indian wars offered the Puritans a new "errand" that would regenerate and reunify the colony, and later, the new nation. To the Puritans, the tribal warriors were not human enemies, but the devil's own soldiers. Therefore, the Indian wars were holy wars, sacred events in the cosmic struggle between good and evil. In taking up arms, the Puritans and their descendants reaffirmed their spiritual mission to claim the wilderness for God. If dispossessing the natives also helped to enrich the Puritans, then this was a sign of God's approval.

"Definition by repudiation," in Slotkin's phrase, also permitted Americans simultaneously to imitate and to reject the alien but attractive culture.[35] The Indian wars justified acts of savagery against the "savage." In fact, the most effective Indian fighters were the hunters, men who had learned the ways of their enemies in order to defeat them.

The Myth of the Frontier was expressed through popular literary genres, especially two of the earliest: the captivity and hunter narratives. In both, the lone protagonist enters the wilderness, voluntarily or involuntarily, encounters its inhabitants, suffers, and at last returns to regenerate her or his community. In the semi-fictional captivity narrative, a colonist, usually a woman, is kidnapped by Indians and forced to live among them. Her suffering in the wilderness strengthens her faith, and her eventual homecoming inspires her community. In the most popular version of the many stories of the hunter, a white loner skilled in the ways of the wilderness simultaneously rescues a white woman and saves civilization from the Indians. In these and later variations, from *Shane* to *Star Wars*, the ending reunites both the personal and communal families.

Even after the secularization of the political community, to be an American was to have what Puritan scholar Sacvan Bercovitch called "a civic identity rooted in a prophetic view of history."[36] America became a city on a hill, a model of democracy.

Such a civic identity is both positive and negative. As political scientist Michael Rogin has shown, Americans defined themselves in opposition to others, beginning with Native Americans and African American slaves, and then, at various points in American history, including women, the poor, immigrants, Latinos,

Asians, Communists, international terrorists, and so on.[37] The endless "wars" against "aliens" allowed the nation to regenerate itself, over and over again.

The Frontier Myth survived the closing of the actual frontier, near the end of the late-nineteenth century, by being transformed into the legend of the "Last Stand." Loosely based on the defeat of General George Custer's army in the Battle of Little Big Horn, in 1876, the Last Stand legend transformed an inept soldier, a mediocre land speculator, and a first-rate self-promoter into a sacrificial hero whose death brought his divided country together. This post-Frontier Myth underscored the bleak possibility that the forces of good might be defeated, thereby justifying the subjugation of potential rebels at home and abroad.[38]

By the turn of the century, the national mission was seen to require international action. But, without the use of force, the city on a hill was too faint a beacon to other nations. So, America had to fight foreign wars to make "the world...safe for democracy," and, incidentally, to expand her own empire.[39]

The story is still going on, the national mission can never be completed, the devil can never be vanquished, the reunification can never be permanent. Final victory, or defeat, would destroy the essential basis of American identity.

Although one emphasizes the individual and the other the community, the stories of the self-made man and the national mission have been complementary. No "self" is ever fully "made," just as the national mission is never over. Even the more successful individuals need a civic as well as a personal identity. Moreover, the national mission to tame the wilderness helped to legitimize territorial expansion, which created more opportunities for individual advancement. The Frontier Myth has also eased, somewhat, the frustrations of those who fail to make themselves, by extending to them membership in the successful nation. As advanced capitalism reduces still further the opportunities for the individual to succeed on his own, the image of the independent, white male defender of civilization remains a comforting fantasy.

In theory at least, the dominant American narrative promotes a kind of democracy. If all Americans share equal membership in the nation and have equal opportunities for economic achievement, then the composite story of the self-made men and their national mission is democratic, if not participatory. But the narrative disguises the extent to which both the men and their country have been "made" at the expense of others. Nearly all of the land claimed by the pioneers was stolen from Native Americans and Mexicans. From the first, the most successful American Adams profited from the labor of poor whites, black slaves, and American "Eves."

Moreover, the American national mission

encourages a far more intrusive government than the limited one designed only to protect the self-made men from each other. Throughout American history, federal and state agencies have played leading roles in repressing internal and external "aliens," including censoring their mail and their publications, spying on their organizations, calling out the army to put down their demonstrations, and legislating, ordering, and enforcing such clear violations of the Constitution as the Jim Crow laws and the internment of Japanese Americans in concentration camps during World War II.[40]

Throughout American history, those on the receiving end of the national mission have been denied basic democratic rights, including the right to vote for which Fannie Lou Hamer struggled, as well as access to the social and economic resources needed for effective political involvement.

Patriotic Resistance

During the Gulf War, Keith Mather, a Vietnam veteran, tried to explain his decision to protest both wars: "I never really thought of myself as patriotic until I started to resist, and I realized I'm just doing what comes naturally to Americans."[41] Mather suggests that political dissidents are the true American patriots. Is this America?

Throughout our history, there has been a

counternarrative often hidden, that redefines American identity and encourages participatory politics. The Puritans' idea of the covenant points the way toward a civic identity based not on repudiation of others, but on shared membership in a community dedicated to realizing its ideals in the world. Although Puritan politics were neither fully participatory nor democratic, the act of covenanting became a political model of mutual commitment to collective action. In the covenant, who we are or are not is less meaningful than who we are trying to become. As John Schaar puts it, a covenant "is not a static legacy, a gift outright, but a burden and a promise."[42]

In the American counternarrative, the key political event is neither the drafting of the Constitution nor the conquest of the wilderness, but the signing of the Declaration of Independence. Its conclusion, "... we mutually pledge to each other our Lives, our Fortunes and our sacred Honor," is an act of covenanting. During this country's greatest crisis of national identity, the Civil War, President Abraham Lincoln articulated a vision of a democratic covenant. What identified and united Americans, from the Daughters of the American Revolution to the most recent immigrants, was not their "blood," but their shared claim to the heritage of the founders:

> We have besides these men—descended by blood from our
> ancestors—among us perhaps half our people who are not

descendants at all.... If they look back through this history to trace their connection with those days by blood, they find they have none, they can not carry themselves back into that glorious epoch and make themselves feel that they are part of us, but when they look through that old Declaration of Independence, they find that those bold men say "We hold these truths to be self-evident, that all men are created equal," and then they feel that that moral sentiment taught in that day evidences their relation to these men, that it is the father of all moral principle in them, and that they have a right to claim it as though they were blood of the blood....[44]

Lincoln knew that the nation's founders had not lived up to their own moral principles. Thomas Jefferson, the author of the Declaration of Independence, was himself a slave owner, and the Constitution recognized slavery. So, it was up to the Civil War generation, those who descended directly from the founders and those who had just arrived, to continue the democratic struggle for equality: "So I say in relation to the principle that all men are created equal, let it be as nearly reached as we can."[45]

Striving together to reach the standard of equality is democratic in a double sense: it is inclusive rather than exclusive, since all have the right to claim it "as though they were blood of the blood"; and it is participatory, since the goal can only be reached through the collective action of all Americans.

The definitive statement of Lincoln's vision of democracy is the Gettysburg Address, which generations of American students have memorized without being aware of its potentially revolutionary content. Lincoln reminds us that honoring the memories of the Civil War dead, and the founders before them, means much more than building monuments or making speeches: "It is for us the living, rather, to be dedicated here to the unfinished work... —that this nation, under God, shall have a new birth of freedom—and that government of the people, by the people, for the people, shall not perish from the earth."[46]

Like the founders, Lincoln and his generation failed to live up to the democratic covenant. Lincoln himself vacillated on the issue of equality between the races; during the Lincoln-Douglas debates, he referred to the inferiority of the blacks, and as President, he suggested that the freed slaves should leave to establish a colony in South America.[47] After Lincoln's death and the brief era of Reconstruction, Southern blacks were stripped of their new political rights, and reduced to the status of sharecroppers, economically dependent on their former masters. Lincoln's suggestion of a more participatory politics was soon absorbed by the dominant American narrative. The assassinated President became this nation's greatest martyr, whose sacrificial death saved us from having to save ourselves.

Yet the counternarrative was never forgotten completely, resurfacing throughout American history, in the political movements that have protested America's lack of democracy in the name of America's democratic ideal. In Richard Flacks's view, "the left has had more meaning in the United States as a cultural than as a political force."[48] Each democratic movement has contributed to keeping alive the collective memory and experience of participatory politics. The civil rights movement and the New Left attempted to recall the nation to its genuine mission: acting together to achieve the "true" democracy that would, in Fannie Lou Hamer's words, "raise me and that white man up...raise America up." In urging all Americans to join the work of "bringing the entire nation back to the wells of democracy that were dug deep by the founding fathers," Martin Luther King echoed Lincoln's call to strive together toward the moral standards that the founders had failed to reach.[49] By requiring each generation to act anew, the sixties interpretation of the American mission encouraged participatory politics.

Actually, the sixties movements invoked themes from both the dominant American narrative and the democratic counternarrative. It is important to bear in mind that the conventional politics of the sixties, against which the young activists rebelled, also recapitulated the basic American story of the holy war that regenerates the nation. John Kennedy's 1960 Presidential campaign slogan, the "New Frontier," recalled earlier journeys into the wilderness, the space program, which he endorsed so enthusiastically, extended the wilderness into outer space. In foreign policy, the new "superpower" justified its various interventions into the affairs of other nations, including Kennedy's disastrous invasion of Cuba at the Bay of Pigs, on the basis of the Cold War against the latest devil, the Soviet Union.

In response, the sixties movements adopted the structure of the conventional American narrative, but gave new content to its traditional components: the national mission, the alien enemy, and the dream of reunification. In proposing a new "agenda for a generation," the young founders of SDS were continuing, self-consciously or not, the American tradition of defying tradition. Their version of the national mission saw the United States a model for alternative politics. The Puritan image of a city on a hill resonates in James Lawson's claim, at SNCC's founding conference, that "The extent to which the Negro, joined by many others, apprehends and incorporates non-violence determines the degree that the world will acknowledge fresh social insight from America."[50]

Although the sixties story was more inclusive than the original version, the problem with this image is the potential separation between the bearers of the mission and those for whom they bear it. If the world looks toward the city on a hill for enlightenment, the city dwellers may come to believe that they have nothing significant to learn from the world. During the late sixties, the privilege and responsibility implicit in the idea of a model community may have contributed to the turn away from participatory democracy, as rival sects competed to annoint themselves as *the* vanguard party in charge of making the revolution on behalf of the less enlightened.

The emphasis on the self-transformation of the organizers and the organized echoed the conventional theme of the self-made man, even though radical self-transformation presupposed rejecting conventional definitions of self, including the assumption of white maleness. Moreover, "self-making" during the sixties was not intrinsically competitive. From Bob Moses, Unita Blackwell learned that "I can stand myself," an example of self-transformation meant to be shared with others.

Many of the sixties activists reenacted the classic American journey into the wilderness, although with a twist. Having grown up in middle-class suburbs, they felt a sense of being trapped by their own affluence and status, as expressed in the oft-repeated opening of The Port Huron Statement, that "We are people of this generation, bred in at least modest comfort, housed in universities, looking uncomfortably to the world we inherit."[51] By venturing into the rural South or the inner city of the North, they entered areas of the country that, in comparison to the 'burbs were wildernesses. Here, they encountered people who were less "civilized," in terms of formal education and material possessions, but who seemed to be more "authentic" and even more free in some ways.[52] As in the familiar American narratives, the sixties heroes suffered and sacrificed, enduring subsistence living, arrests, beatings, and the murders of their companions, in order to redeem and reunify America.

The sixties movements also fought against their own versions of the devil, with negative consequences. Asked to explain the decline of the civil rights movement during the late sixties, James Farmer, the former leader of the Congress on Racial Equality (CORE), observed that "It's difficult to organize around a campaign when you don't have a devil." In the first part of the decade, civil rights activists were united in opposition to clear enemies: the white racists who defended segregation. But later on, the absence of a "devil" led to debilitating internal divisions: "We had to fight somebody so we fought each other."[53] In both the civil rights movement and the New Left, the emphasis shifted from what Americans shared to what divided them, from the national mission as mutual commitment to democracy to the national mission as holy war. By the end of the decade the struggle against the devil had come to justify racial separatism and revolutionary violence.

Even as apocalypse began to seem ever more likely, the participants in the sixties movements dreamed of national reunification, just as their ancestors did. The sixties movements offered alternative visions of perfect harmony. SNCC was conceived as a "band of brothers, standing in a circle of love," while each ERAP project tried to become the equivalent of a "happy family," and to provide "the extraordinary intimacy experienced by people who have fallen in love." Ironically, the dream of perfect unity made it harder to accept and resolve the conflicts that inevitably arise within families and among lovers, and more difficult to resist the pressures to identify the movement with a single leader, even one as unwilling to be so identified as Bob "Moses."

Even those who rejected nearly every premise of the national story retained its framework, while reversing its terms. To Malcolm X, "what is to them an American dream is to us an American nightmare." The United States was even seen as a negative city on a hill. To SNCC organizer Charles Cobb, "America must be treated as an enemy—an enemy to humanity in fact, and cut loose from."[54]

The influence of the basic American narrative hindered as well as helped the sixties efforts to reclaim democracy. Criticizing America in the name of its ideals inspired the formation of SNCC and SDS, and helped them to reach many potential new members and supporters. However, the conventional American story also weakened the movements, by distracting attention from the teaching and practice of participatory politics. The sixties activists were caught in the same bind as the great writers of the American Renaissance described by Sacvan Bercovitch: "The dream that inspired them to defy the false Americanism of their time compelled them to speak their defiance as keepers of the dream."[55]

"A Filthy, Obscene Memory"?

Today, both the critics and the defenders of the sixties speak as keepers of the dream. The positive and the negative stories we tell ourselves about the sixties recapitulate the basic American narrative of the national mission against the aliens, on which depends the fate not only of America, but the world.

In the "official," negative memory, America struggled to defend itself from the forces of chaos and totalitarianism masquerading as democratic movements. The defeat of the sixties movements proved that this country remains a city on a hill, or as journalist Michael Barone puts it, a "model of the world." The positive memory of the sixties also tells of a national mission with international consequences, but in this version, America stands for participatory politics at home and abroad. During the sixties, activists tried to recover and extend the "true" democracy that has inspired democrats everywhere.

In both the negative and positive stories of the sixties, demonic legions threaten to overwhelm the nation. The negative story rests on a stark division between devils and saints. There is Lucifer himself: Malcolm X, along with secondary fiends, including Huey Newton of the Black Panthers and Tom Hayden of SDS (although Malcolm himself has been undergoing something of a cultural rehabilitation). Their followers, the movement participants, have been dehumanized and inflated into gun-toting Black Panthers, crazed Chicago rioters, braless women's libbers, and lewd hippies, all of whom titillate as well as threaten. Collier and Horowitz actually describe the New Left as a rejuvenated horror film monster.

The most dangerous agents of the devil today are the former sixties activists who have not had second thoughts. The words used to disparage the latest aliens—"infantile," "irrational," "cruel," "sick"—echo earlier characterizations of Native Americans, African Americans, workers, women, immigrants. The term "the sixties" has itself become shorthand for "alien." During the Gulf War, the *New York Times* effectively dismissed the demonstrators against the war by associating them with "the aura of the 60's." References such as "shaggy youths pounding on tom-toms" evoke the Indian enemies of the past; "fringe groups" implies that the protestors are deviants; and "angry language about

American imperialism and racism" suggests that criticism of foreign policy or race relations is irrational, beyond the bounds of civilized discourse.

The struggle between good and evil is also the main plot of the positive story of the sixties. The search for a devil to blame for the end of the sixties tends to upstage the vision of collective action for democracy. Prime candidates for arch-fiend are Presidents Johnson and Nixon. Other figures in the diabolic pantheon are Chicago Mayor Richard Daley, who unleashed his police force against the demonstrators outside the Democratic Convention; Birmingham Sheriff "Bull" Connor, who turned fire hoses and vicious dogs on Martin Luther King and the nonviolent marchers; and FBI Chief J. Edgar Hoover, who authorized wiretaps, infiltrations, and other repressive tactics against the civil rights movement and the New Left.

The sympathetic sixties narrative sees devils within, as well as outside the movements, such as the Black Power extremists who "destroyed" SNCC, and the fanatical revolutionaries who "destroyed" SDS. No matter who plays the leading villain(s) in the struggle between the "good" and "bad" sixties, the devil triumphs in the end.

Both the negative and positive stories of the sixties promise that redoubled effort will lead to national regeneration. As in earlier American narratives, the nation is compared to a family, divided by the rebellion of children against parents, but reunited at last. In the negative version, nearly all of the youthful rebels came to understand, with the second thoughts, that what they called politics was nothing more than an Oedipal revolt. In the positive version of the sixties, the children had good intentions, rebelling in order to save the nation. But, by the end of the sixties, they also realized that they had gone too far. So, the prodigal sons and daughters return home to their private and public families.

During a 1969 antiwar march organized by the Vietnam Veterans Against the War, one of the speakers anticipated two possible future memories of the sixties. John Kerry urged his fellow vets to undertake one last mission:

> to search and destroy the last vestige of this barbaric war, to pacify our own hearts, to conquer the hate and fear that has driven this country these last ten years and more, so when thirty years from now our brothers go down the street without a leg, without an arm, or a face, and small boys ask why, we will be able to say "Vietnam," and not mean a desert, not a filthy, obscene memory, but mean instead the place where America finally turned and where soldiers like us helped in the turning.[55]

Kerry seemed to propose a new version of the traditional hunter narrative; this time the prey would be the "filthy, obscene" national memory of the Vietnam War era.

But twenty-five years later, the nation has still not "turned." Kerry himself is now a United States senator, but many Vietnam veterans have not been able to turn their lives around, let alone help to turn around the country. The answer to Fannie Lou Hamer's question, "Is this America?" remains contested.

Yet Kerry's prophetic comment reminds us of our own responsibility for the national memory. The best way to answer Hamer's question may be to rephrase it: "What will America be?" Through participatory politics, we can act together to "turn" America into the democracy that it claims to be.

CONCLUSION

RECLAIMING DEMOCRACY

THE first thing I saw when I drove up to the intersection was a double line of trucks stopped in the middle of the road. The trucks were so huge that I couldn't see how far the two rows went back: at least five blocks. Each uncovered flatbed was heaped high with a mountain of garbage. It was noisy: the idling truck engines rattled and clanged; mothers called to the children playing and watching from the sidewalks; a crowd of people off to my left shouted and chanted; scavenger birds cawed. It was smelly, too, with strong odors of exhaust, rotting garbage, smoke, smells that I couldn't place exactly but which reminded me of factories that I'd visited as a union rep. There was dust everywhere, thick enough for kids to have written their names on the windows of the cars parked in the side street where I looked for a parking space. Bits of trash blew in the wind, down the streets, onto the sidewalks, into the tiny yards of the small but well-kept row houses.

I unlocked the doors to let the students out, and watched them run toward the group of about fifty people who were blocking the main gate where the trucks were headed. Behind them I could see the vast incinerator waiting to receive the contents of the trucks, its wide tower billowing dark smoke into the sky. I got out of the car and walked toward the protestors, who carried signs with handwritten slogans such as "No rats! No trucks! No trash!" and "Stop killing us!"

It was hard to believe that this unlikely coalition of elderly Ukrainians, African-American families, and a few college students could have completely shut down the entrance for two hours. Yet, the one police officer on the scene leaned quietly on his car. A student ran up to me, excited: "The CEO is flying out right now! He's agreed to meet with us!"

Known euphemistically as a "resource recovery facility," the site for the Westinghouse trash incinerator had been chosen in 1987, without input from the residents, few of whom even heard about the single public hearing. Yet the trash-to-steam plant, one of the largest in the country, would be located only 80 feet from the closest homes in the West End neighborhood of Chester, Pennsylvania. Since 1991, when the incinerator opened, trucks with New York, Delaware, and Ohio license plates barreled down Thurlow Street, once a quiet residential road, six days each week, often fifteen or more hours a day.

The noise kept sleepy children awake until late at night, and woke them early the next morning. Their parents swept the dust that invaded their homes, and tried to get rid of the trash that flew off the heavily loaded, uncovered trucks, before it attracted the rats which had arrived with the incinerator. Mothers and grandmothers watched their children as carefully as they could, to catch them before they chased a ball into the street where the trucks rattled by. Many noticed that they were coughing more, and that their kids seemed to be missing more days of school because of illness. A few neighbors began to ask questions about the chemicals spewed into the air by the huge smokestack next door. Finally, they came together to form a neighborhood action organization, Chester Residents Concerned for Quality Living, which organized the rally.[1]

Through their new political experiences, from demonstrations to public hearings, the members of CRCQL have learned that their fight against the incinerator in their neighborhood is part of a nation-wide struggle against what has come to be called environmental racism. Industries which pollute or are otherwise undesirable are often sited in relatively powerless communities of poor people especially people of color.

Chester, for example, is a typical Northeast city that declined rapidly when its main industry, the shipyards that lined the river where the incinerator is now, relocated overseas. As whites fled to the suburbs, the population of the city declined precipitously, while the proportion of African Americans and the unemployed rose. Chester is now one of the most depressed cities in Pennsylvania, with a school district that ranks at the very bottom of the 501 districts in the state. Until 1991, however, the city was controlled by a Republican machine; as recently as 1992, Swarthmore students helping to register voters encountered people who told them that they had never been able to register as Democrats because they worked for the city. Today, four years after the first Democratic majority was elected to the Chester City Council, the city continues to struggle against the same economic and political conditions that threaten much larger cities with more resources and longer histories of empowerment.[2]

Yet despite the many obstacles, the members of CRCQL have achieved important victories through participatory action. As a result of the truck blockade, they did have their first opportunity to tell their story to the Chief Executive Officer of Westinghouse. In response, the company built a new road for the trucks hauling trash to the incinerator. While the noise and dust have decreased, the new route is still only a block away. Meanwhile, the residents have become very concerned about the less visible, but more dangerous problem of exposure to chemical pollutants. Working with other community organizations, CRCQL helped to convince the Chester City Council to pass a resolution against the siting of any new industry that would increase pollution. But the incinerator is still there, and so the struggle goes on.

Zulene Mayfield, whose house faces the incinerator, is the chairperson of CRCQL. She's a charismatic speaker and self-taught organizer who knows the name of every person in a room within a minute or two of walking through the door. Somehow she manages to put hours into CRCQL every day while holding down a full-time job and helping out her family. Although she was just a little girl during the sixties, she was inspired by her mother's participation in the civil rights movement (today, Mrs. Mayfield would not miss a CRCQL rally). Zulene says:

> Historically, black people haven't realized the power they have. The people who have realized it, who have the knowledge, have to teach the others. We have to start using our power.[3]

Like Chester Residents Concerned for Quality Living, people in neighborhoods and workplaces thoughout the country are practicing participatory politics. Some, like Zulene Mayfield, are aware of the democratic tradition which they are helping to carry on; others have yet to realize "the power they have." Beneath the negative national memory of the sixties is story that could help all of us to reclaim democracy.

We Are All Leaders

Why insist on the importance of remembering the country's most recent experiments in participatory politics, if they simply prove, once again, that this kind of democracy is ephemeral at best?

Unpacking the popular sixties slogan, "we are all leaders," reveals hard questions about the feasibility and desirability of participatory politics.

Recovering the story of the civil rights movement and the New Left means recovering the *whole* story. The sixties made a difference, especially the defeat of legal segregation, the ending of the Vietnam War, and the participation of many ordinary Americans in politics. But the movements did not bring about the "true" democracy. Poverty and discrimination persist, military interventions continue, and the vast majority of the people are resigned, if cynical, about their passive roles in the political system.

"We"

Who "are all leaders"? Reclaiming democracy requires addressing the difficult issue of who participates. We can begin by rejecting the historic approach of conventional American politics, definition by repudiation. In a democracy, who we are must be more than who we are *not*. But, then, what is the positive definition that unites us?

Also, how many are "we"? If only a small number of people can participate at one time, as the sixties experience suggests, then what political structures could link local democratic communities to each other? In contemporary politics, the decision-making that affects our collective lives occurs in a variety of settings, from the shop floor to the floor of the Senate, from a local neighborhood to a multinational corporation. Each of us belongs to multiple, overlapping "we's." How can we participate in more than one community, in a nation, in the world?

At their best, the sixties movements brought people of different races and backgrounds together on the basis of a common project: the struggle for democracy.

It is possible to sustain this kind of unity? SNCC and SDS were unable to do so, retreating to the negative politics which they had opposed. What political institutions would enable us to define ourselves positively, through democratic action?

"Are"

The question, "Who are we?" is intertwined with two others, "Who were we?" and "Who will we be?" All of us are not leaders now and have rarely ever been so in the past. Reclaiming democracy involves coming to terms with the obstacles to real political change. How do people become aware of the possibility of greater participation in politics, and what enables them to act on that awareness?

During the sixties, many Southerners and Northerners learned to "stand" themselves, through the examples of SNCC and the ERAP project of SDS. But the activists also struggled over the best way to grow and sustain their movements: Should SNCC and SDS have become more like organizations or more like movements? Should they have focused on political or cultural change? Should they have concentrated on prefiguring the participatory politics which is their goal, or have done whatever is most strategic, regardless of democracy? Today, how can participatory politics be encouraged in the face of hostile national governments and international corporations, when the democratic past and present are almost invisible?

"All"

Reclaiming democracy today requires facing up to the fact that contemporary politics pulls us apart, instead of bringing us together. Afraid of the present and cynical about the future, we cling to racial, religious, class, and many other identities, barely able to conceive that a broader "we" could *all* be anything, let alone "leaders." Even those who still believe in the dream of greater democracy are often isolated in their own free spaces or organized into separate feminist, environmental, peace, gay and lesbian, student, labor, civil rights, and other movements, not to mention groups within these movements.

The comparatively broad sixties movements also became fragmented, despite or because of the unrealistic expectation that politics ought to be "a circle of love." But democracy should not be confused with harmony. If there were neither differences nor conflicts, there would be no need for politics. So, how can participatory democracy reconcile unity and diversity, identity politics and coalition-building?

"Leaders"

How would a democracy in which "we are all leaders" actually work? Reclaiming democracy means taking a hard look at the meaning of democratic leadership. Can we all be leaders? If we are all leaders, then perhaps no one is. Do all of us even want to be leaders? The attempts of the sixties movements to do away with leadership tended to produce unaccountable leaders instead. Yet, there were also leaders, such as Bob Moses, who enabled the Unita Blackwells to develop their own capacities for leadership. Perhaps, instead of a dichotomy between leadership and participation, there is actually a reciprocal relationship between leaders and participants in democracy. How can leaders empower some of us to become leaders, and all of us to participate in politics?

Retelling the full story of the sixties will not resolve the question of the feasibility and desirability of participatory politics. The purpose of this book has been to remove one of the chief obstacles to an answer: the selective, distorted memory of the latest national moment of participatory politics. As difficult as reclaiming the tradition and practice of democracy will be, what alternative is there to trying? Acquiescing in injustice? As activist and scholar, I do not see how the crises of racism, poverty, and despair can be solved without greater democracy.

Even its advocates tend to view political participation negatively, as something we *ought* rather than want to do. Unless obligation, oppression, or guilt drives us into politics, we are inclined to agree with

Oscar Wilde's famous observation that, to paraphrase, the trouble with politics is that it takes too many evenings. However, American political thinking has almost totally missed the secret discovered by the Chester demonstrators who blocked the trucks: that political participation can be meaningful, fulfilling, and simply, fun.

Through participation, we become more fully who we are, as individuals *and* as members of communities. Through participation, we become political adults, making decisions together about our collective lives. Through participation, we share in a movement culture of preparing meals together, of telling stories, of singing great songs (I know from personal experience that there's a place on the picket line for the worst of voices), of being connected to a particular group of people, and to the activists who came before and who will come after us.

If Hannah Arendt's descriptive phrase, "joy in action," seems deluded or self-indulgent, think of your own experience: the excitement of walking as a group into a hearing room to protest the closing of the neighborhood school, the satisfaction of putting together a childcare cooperative, the bond between you and others after a difficult workplace issue has been talked through and resolved. Of course, political experiences also include the tensions and passions inevitable when we come together to deliberate and decide issues that really matter.

If you don't have experience, go out and get some; participation is a learned activity, like riding a bike. The more you practice, the better you get, and the more you appreciate and enjoy it. If your political experience is still too frustrating, make it better, or wear a helmet. Unless we live as hermits, we already participate, if only in the most passive sense, as complacent or disgruntled spectators.

In fact, the real choice before the nation may not be between participation and acquiescence, but between democratic and undemocratic participation. Many people today participate in the resurgent Christian Right, but how democratic is a movement for hierarchy and intolerance? Meanwhile, the disturbances in Los Angeles following the Rodney King verdict indicate that people who have been excluded from the political and economic systems may express their frustration by "participating" in a riot. Yet, these developments also suggest that people *do* want to participate in politics, but don't know how. If the national memory included the lost tradition of democratic participation, perhaps Americans would see the possibility of reclaiming democracy.

Discovering Our Past for Ourselves
One of the most popular movies of 1994, *Forrest Gump*, recapitulates the dominant memory of the sixties, one

chapter in the story of recent American history as told by a kindly simpleton. The New Left is represented by a dirty, long-haired fanatic, who beats Forrest's true love, Jenny. Hovering in the background are the stand-ins for the civil rights movement: loud, cartoonish Black Panther-types with guns. The audience cheers when Forrest punches out the SDS leader, in an unsuccessful attempt to rescue Jenny. There is only a single passing reference to the women's movement, when Forrest is jogging back and forth across America.

The movie retells the classic American story of the redemptive hero, updated for the nineties. Forrest's heroism is strangely passive; he reacts to situations which he does not understand by taking action, sometimes violent. Yet he always saves the day, preserving America from its latest assailants, including the sixties activists. Jenny succumbs to AIDS (implicitly because she was corrupted by the free-love philosophy of the sixties), but Forrest will carry on as both father and mother to their son, the next Forrest Gump. Forrest personifies the ideal American citizen in the nineties; uninterested in and incapable of political participation, but always ready and able to defend his country and his woman.

Can a movement for democratic change draw inspiration from an undemocratic past? Can the story of the few democratic moments in American history really contribute to the project of reclaiming democracy? Only if we follow Hannah Arendt's advice, to discover our past for ourselves. Our selective, negative memory of the sixties has largely hidden America's most recent national experience of participatory politics. But rediscovering that experience should not mean simply reenacting it.

To reclaim the full memory of the sixties is to reclaim a question, not an answer, a possibility, not a guarantee. As an activist, I hope to help make America as democratic as it claims to be. As an author, I hope that this book will help to put the issue of participatory politics back on the national political agenda. Ultimately, however, the meaning of democracy will be decided through politics, not memory. Right now, in neighborhoods, workplaces, and on campuses, Americans are participating in politics, as they have done throughout their history. Reclaiming the sixties is only one step toward reclaiming democracy.

NOTES

Preface: *"The Thread of Hopeful Memory"*

1 Quoted in Maureen Dowd, "G.O.P.'s Rising Star Pledges to Right the Wrongs of the Left," *New York Times*, November 10, 1994.

2 Dowd, "G.O.P.'s Rising Star." In orders to make this book as accessible as possible, I have followed the conventional usage of the term, "American" politics, to refer to the politics of the United States. I recognize, however, that "America" includes all of North, Central, and South America, and that its use as a synonym for the United States is offensive, rightly, to many people.

3 In this book, I use both the terms, "black" and "African American," following conventional usages in this community. The farmworkers from Mexico with whom I have worked prefer generally to be called Mexicans, no matter how long they have been in this country. These terms are often controversial and change frequently; I apologize for any offense that my choices may have given.

4 Nadinne Cruz, Lang Professor of Social Change, Swarthmore College. Personal communication, Spring, 1993.

5 Hannah Arendt, *Crises of the Republic* (New York: Harcourt Brace Jovanovich, 1972), 206.

6 See Harry C. Boyle, *The Backyard Revolution: Understanding the New Citizen Movement* (Philadelphia: Temple University Press, 1980) and *CommonWealth: A Return to Citizen Politics* (New York: Free Press, 1989).

One: *Remembering Democracy*

1 *Phoenix*, November 16, 1963.

2 *Phoenix*, November 23, 1963.

3 Quoted in "Swarthmore Collegians Ripped For Roles in Chester

Protests," *Philadelphia Daily News*, November 22, 1963.

4 Maureen Gray and Margaret Kraus, "Letters to the Editor," *Chester, Pennsylvania Times*, November 26, 1963.

5 *Phoenix*, November 23, 1963.

6 *Phoenix*, November 16, 1963.

7 On the bombing, see Kirkpatrick Sale, *SDS* (New York: Vintage Books, 1974), 3–6.

8 George F. Will, "Slamming the Doors," *Newsweek* (March 25, 1991), 66.

9 Will, *Newsweek*, 66.

10 Quoted in Herbert Mitgang, "Books of the Times: Trying to Reactivate America's Liberal Impulse," *New York Times*, March 17, 1992.

11 On the Vietnam syndrome, see Maureen Dowd, "White House Memo: War Introduces Nation to a Tougher Bush," *New York Times*, March 2, 1991, and Jane Gross, "The Vietnam Generation Surrenders Its Certainty," *New York Times*, January 15, 1991.

12 On the status of women, see Naomi Wolf, *The Beauty Myth: How Images of Beauty Are Used Against Women* (New York: William Morrow, 1991), 134, and Diane Johnson, "Something for the Boys," *New York Review of Books*, January 16, 1992, 13. On the state of the labor movement, see Thomas Geoghegan, *Which Side Are You On? Trying to Be for Labor When It's Flat on Its Back* (New York: Farrar, Strauss, & Giroux, 1991), 15.

13 See Michael Wines, "White House Links Riots to Welfare," *New York Times*, May 5, 1992, and Andrew Rosenthal, "Quayle Says Riots Arose From Burst of Social Anarchy," *New York Times*, May 20, 1992.

14 See Paul Berman, *Debating P.C.: The Controversy Over Political Correctness on College Campuses* (New York: Dell, Laurel, 1992); Dinesh D'Souza, *Illiberal Education: The Politics of Race and Gender on Campus* (New York: Free Press, Macmillan, Inc., 1991); Roger Kimball, *Tenured Radicals: How Politics Has Corrupted Our Higher Education* (New York: Harper & Row, 1990).

15 Thomas Pynchon, *Vineland* (Boston: Little, Brown, 1990); Marylouise Oates, *Making Peace* (New York: Warner Books, 1991). On the revival of sixties fashion, see Nina Darnton, "Lifestyle: Not-So-Groovy

Threads," *Newsweek*, March 25, 1991, 63; of sixties fragrances, see Elaine Louie, "Some Scents of the 60's Are Wafting Again," *New York Times*, January 22, 1992; and of sixties rock and roll, see Gene Santoro, "Music: Rockin' in the Free World," *The Nation* March 11, 1991, 318.

16 Taylor Branch, *Parting the Waters: America in the King Years 1954–63* (New York: Simon and Schuster, 1988); Elaine Brown, *A Taste of Power: A Black Woman's Story* (New York: Pantheon, 1992); Peter Collier and David Horowitz, *Destructive Generation: Second Thoughts About the Sixties* (New York: Summit Books, 1989); Todd Gitlin, *The Sixties: Years of Hope, Days of Rage* (New York: Bantam Books, 1987); James Miller, "*Democracy Is in the Streets*": *From Port Huron to the Siege of Chicago* (New York: Simon and Schuster, A Touchstone Book, 1987). Other important books are: Wini Breines, *Community and Organization in the New Left, 1962–1968: The Great Refusal*, 2d ed. (New Brunswick: Rutgers University Press, 1989); David Caute, *The Year of the Barricades: A Journey Through 1968* (New York: Perennial Library, Harper & Row, 1988); David Farber, *Chicago '68* (Chicago: University of Chicago Press, 1988); Gerald Howard, ed., *The Sixties: Arts, Politics, and Media of our Most Explosive Decade*, 2d ed. (New York: Paragon House, 1991); Maurice Isserman, *If I Had a Hammer: The Death of the Old Left and the Birth of the New Left* (New York: Basic Books, 1987); George Katsiaficas, *The Imagination of the New Left: A Global Analysis of 1968* (Boston: South End Press, 1987); Mary King, *Freedom Song: A Personal Story of the 1960s Civil Rights Movement* (New York: William Morrow, Quill, 1987); Sohnya Sayers et al., *The 60s Without Apology* (Minneapolis: University of Minnesota Press, in cooperation with *Social Text*, 1984).

17 Lorraine Ali, "Kurt Cobain Screamed Out Our Angst," *New York Times*, April 17, 1994.

18 R.W. Apple, Jr., "A Passion Spent, Finally," *New York Times*, February 4, 1994.

19 Clayborne Carson, *In Struggle: SNCC and the Black Awakening of the 1960s* (Cambridge, MA: Harvard University Press, 1981); Mary King,

Freedom Song.

20 Barbie Zelizer, *Covering the Body: The Kennedy Assassination, the Media, and the Shaping of Collective Memory* (Chicago: University of Chicago Press, 1992); Michael Schudson, *Watergate in American memory: how we remember, forget, and reconstruct the past* (New York: Basic Books, 1992).

21 Quoted in Henry Kamm, "Spirit of 1968 Is Still Alive, Still Distinct," *New York Times*, November 30, 1989.

22 John Tagliabue, "Prague Turns on Those Who Brought the 'Spring,'" *New York Times*, February 24, 1992.

23 See Hanna Fenichal Pitkin, *Fortune is a Woman: Gender and Politics in the Thought of Nicolo Machiavelli* (Berkeley: University of California Press, 1984), 289.

24 Karen Palermo, quoted in Roberto Suro, "Viewing Chaos in the Capital, Americans Express Outrage," *New York Times*, October 19, 1990.

25 Bernard R. Berelson, Paul F. Lazarsfeld, and William N. McPhee, *Voting* (Chicago: University of Chicago Press, 1954), 314–15.

26 Joseph A. Schumpeter, *Capitalism, Socialism, and Democracy*, 3rd ed. (New York: Harper Torchbooks, 1976), 283, 285.

27 See Benjamin Barber, *Strong Democracy: Participatory Politics for a New Age* (Berkeley: University of California Press, 1984); Joshua Cohen and Joel Rogers, *On Democracy: Toward a Transformation of American Society* (New York: Penguin Books, 1986); Phillip Green, *Retrieving Democracy: In Search of Civic Equality* (Totowa, NJ: Rowan and Allanheld, 1985).

28 Quoted in Daniel Singer, "Letter From Europe," *The Nation*, June 20, 1994, 863.

29 Richard Slotkin, *The Fatal Environment: The Myth of the Frontier in the Age of Industrialization, 1800–1890* (Middletown, CT: Wesleyan University Press, 1986), 25.

30 Quoted in Henry Rousso, *The Vichy Syndrome: History and Memory in France since 1944*, trans. Arthur Goldhammer, 2d rev. ed. (Cambridge: Harvard University Press, 1991), 5.

31 Rousso, *The Vichy Syndrome* 4. The field of the history of memory is

influenced strongly by psychoanalysis, as suggested by the title of Rousso's book. For American readers, this title may evoke the "Vietnam Syndrome." See also Michael Paul Rogin on the "cultural impulse to have the experience and not to retain it in memory." Michael Paul Rogin, "'Make My Day!'" *Representations* 29 (Winter 1990): 107.

32 Pierre Nora, "Between Memory and History: Les Lieux de Memoire," *Representations* 26 (Spring 1989): 7.

33 Nora, "Between Memory and History," 7.

34 Hannah Arendt, "The Crisis in Culture," in *Between Past and Future: Eight Exercises in Political Thought*, new and enl. ed. (New York: The Viking Press, 1968) 204.

35 Karl Marx, "The Eighteenth Brumaire of Louis Bonaparte," in Robert C. Tucker, ed. *The Marx-Engels Reader* (New York: W. W. Norton and Company, 1978), 439.

36 Arendt, "Truth and Politics," in *Between Past and Future*, 258.

37 Slotkin, *Fatal Environment*, 20. See Hayden White on the difficulty of obtaining a purely historical account of reality, in *Metahistory: The Historical Imagination in Nineteenth-Century Europe* (Baltimore: The Johns Hopkins University Press, 1974), 21.

38 The sources of political and popular culture that have been most helpful include the books, films, trends, etc. referenced in the endnotes #9–15, in addition to print and electronic media. As the national "paper of record," the *New York Times* has been a major source for the "official" memory of the sixties.

Two: *"The True Democracy"*

1 Quoted in Juan Williams, *Eyes on the Prize: America's Civil Rights Years, 1954–65* (New York: Penguin Books, 1988), 244.

2 Quoted in Stewart Burns, *Social Movements of the 1960s: Searching for Democracy* (Boston: Twayne Publishers, 1990), 13. On the history of SNCC, see Carson, *In Struggle*; Branch, *Parting the Waters*; August Meier, Elliott Rudwick, and Francis L. Broderick, eds., *Black Protest Thought in the Twentieth Century*, 2d ed. (Indianapolis: Bobbs-Merrill, 1971); Mary King, *Freedom Song*.

3 Reverend James Lawson, quoted in Carson, *In Struggle*, 23.

4 Quoted in Gitlin, *The Sixties*, 107.

5 Casey Hayden, "Preface," in Mary King, *Freedom Song*, 7.

6 Quoted in Marilyn Young, *The Vietnam Wars 1945–90* (New York: HarperCollins, 1991), 198.

7 James M. Lawson, Jr., "From a Lunch-Counter Stool," in Meier, Rudnick, and Broderick, *Black Protest Thought*, 314. In this speech, the keynote address to the SNCC founding conference in April 1960, Lawson compared SNCC to the National Association for the Advancement of Colored People (NAACP). In its philosophy of nonviolent action, SNCC resembled the Southern Christian Leadership Conference led by Dr. Martin Luther King, Jr. However, the early SNCC came closer than King's own minister-led organization to putting the philosophy into practice. Later, there were serious disputes between King and SNCC over the latter's increasing militancy, and endorsement of racial separatism and violence.

8 Quoted in Williams, *Eyes on the Prize*, 177.

9 Quoted in Howell Raines, *My Soul Is Rested: Movement Days in the Deep South Remembered* (New York: Penguin Books, 1987), 266.

10 Quoted in Henry Hampton and Steve Fayer, with Karen Flynn, *Voices of Freedom: An Oral History of the Civil Rights Movements from the 1950s through the 1980s.* (New York: Bantam Books, 1991), 59.

11 Quoted in Sara M. Evans and Harry C. Boyte, *Free Spaces: The Sources of Democratic Change in America* (New York: Perennial Library, Harper & Row, 1986), 62. Baker's views differed from those of most of her colleagues at SCLC, including her successor as Executive Director, Wyatt Tee Walker: "I used to have to tell staff, 'Don't call Dr. King "Martin." He's the President, he's our leader. You call him Dr. King around here.'" Quoted in Fred Powledge, *Free At Last? The Civil Rights Movement and the People Who Made It* (Boston: Little, Brown, 1991), 505.

12 Quoted in Carson, *In Struggle*, 303.

13 Quoted in Raines, *My Soul Is Rested*, 240.

14 Quoted in Raines, *My Soul Is Rested*, 237.

15 Casey Hayden, "Preface," in Mary King, *Freedom Song*, 8. Reagon

agrees: "What I can remember is being very alive and very clear, the clearest I've ever been in my life. I knew that every minute I was doing what I was supposed to do." Quoted in Williams, *Eyes on the Prize*, 107.

16 Lawrence Goodwyn, *The Populist Moment: A Short History of the Agrarian Revolt in America* (New York: Oxford University Press, 1978), xix.

17 Quoted in Hampton and Fayer, *Voices of Freedom*, 180.

18 Quoted in Carson, *In Struggle*, 236.

19 James M. Lawson, Jr., "From a Lunch-Counter Stool," 314.

20 Lawson, "from a Lunch-Counter Stool," 307–08.

21 Lawson, "from a Lunch-Counter Stool," 307–08.

22 Quoted in Hampton and Fayer, *Voices of Freedom*, 66.

23 Quoted in Hampton and Fayer, *Voices of Freedom*, 66. For a slightly different account, see Branch, *Parting the Waters*, 295.

24 Bernie Schweid, a white bookstore owner sympathetic to the the sit-in movement, reports: "When Mayor Ben West said, 'Well, in my heart, I have to say I think it's wrong,' that seemed to be a kind of turning point. I think the merchants were afraid to move on their own, were almost looking for an excuse to say, 'Well, if that's what the mayor thinks, then maybe we ought to go ahead.' And they decided to go ahead and start integrating some of the lunch counters. And the sky didn't fall in when that happened." Quoted in Hampton and Fayer, *Voices of Freedom*, 67.

25 Martin Luther King Jr., "Letter From A Birmingham Jail," in *Why We Can't Wait* (New York: A Mentor Book, New American Library, 1964), 94.

26 Bruce Payne, "SNCC: An Overview Two Years Later," in Mitchell Cohen and Dennis Hale, *The New Student Left*, rev. ed. (Boston: Beacon Press, 1967), 90.

27 Quoted in Raines, *My Soul Is Rested*, 240.

28 Charles Sherrod, "SNCC Manual," in Powledge, *Free At Last?*, 343.

29 Mary King and Casey Hayden, "SNCC Position Paper: Women in the Movement," 1964, in Judith Albert and Stewart Albert, eds., *The Sixties Papers: Documents of a Rebellious Decade* (New York:

Prager, 1984), 115.

30 Quoted in Raines, *My Soul is Rested*, 108.

31 Anne Moody, *Coming of Age in Mississippi* (New York: Dell, Laurel, 1968), 319.

32 Moody, *Coming of Age*, 321–22.

33 Mary King, *Freedom Song*, 484. King herself took the "freedom high" position.

34 Mary King, *Freedom Song*, 449.

35 Quoted in Mary King, *Freedom Song*, 447.

36 Quoted in Carson, *In Struggle*, 217.

37 Quoted in Mary King, *Freedom Song*, 497, 503.

38 Chicago Office of SNCC, "WE WANT BLACK POWER," leaflet, 1967, in Meier, Rudnick, and Broderick, *Black Protest Thought*, 487, 489.

39 Chicago Office of SNCC, "WE WANT BLACK POWER," 489.

40 Julius Lester, "The Angry Children of Malcolm X," 1966, in Meier, Rudnick, and Broderick, *Black Protest Thought*, 482.

41 Malcolm X and James Farmer, "Separation or Integration: A Debate," 1962, in Meier, Rudnick, and Broderick, *Black Protest Thought*, 392. Lester also felt that "the Dream was beginning to look like a nightmare," Lester, "Angry Children," 479.

42 Martin Luther King, Jr., "Showdown for Non-Violence," 1968, in Meier, Rudnick, and Broderick, *Black Protest Thought*, 594.

43 Quoted in Carson, *In Struggle*, 224.

44 On SDS/ERAP, see Wini Breines, *Community and Organization*; Stewart Burns, *Social Movements of the 1960s*; Cohen and Hale, eds., *The New Student Left* (Boston: Beacon Press, 1967); Sara M. Evans, *Personal Politics: The Roots of Women's Liberation in the Civil Rights Movement and the New Left* (New York: Vintage Books, 1980); Todd Gitlin, *The Sixties*; Paul Jacobs and Saul Landau, *The New Radicals: A Report with Documents* (New York: Vintage Books, 1966); Miller, *"Democracy Is in the Streets"*; Kirkpatrick Sale, *SDS*.

45 SDS, "The Port Huron Statement," in Judith Clavier Albert and Stewart Albert, *The Sixties Papers*, 176.

46 SDS, "The Port Huron Statement," 181.

47 Quoted in Miller, *Democracy Is in the Streets*, 144.

48 Quoted in Paul Jacobs and Saul Landau, eds. *The New Radicals*, 32.

49 Norman Mailer, *The Armies of the Night*, (New York: Signet Books, 1968), 104.

50 Tom Hayden, "President's Report," in the March–April 1963 *SDS Bulletin*, quoted in Sale, *SDS*, 97.

51 Carl Wittman and Thomas Hayden, "An Interracial Movement of the Poor?" in Cohen and Hale, *New Student Left*, Winter 1963, 175–214.

52 Al Haber, quoted in Miller, *Democracy Is in the Streets*, 190. Haber concluded that "the cult of the ghetto [was] slightly sick." Ibid.

53 ERAP brochure, quoted in Breines, *Community and Organization*, 125.

54 Richie Rothstein, quoted in Breines, *Community and Organization*, 141–2.

55 Quoted in Evans, *Personal Politics*, 136.

56 Andrew Kopkind quoted in Sale, *SDS*, 140.

57 Quoted in Edward P. Morgan, *The 60s Experience: Hard Lessons About Modern America* (Philadelphia: Temple University Press, 1991), 277. Bettina Aptheker, of the Berkeley Free Speech Movement, also remembers "the intense moment of connection between us which infused a spirit of overwhelming and enduring love." Quoted in Burns, *Social Movements of the 1960s*, 64.

58 Statement made to Todd Gitlin and Nanci Hollander, quoted in Sale, *SDS*, 148–9.

59 Gitlin, *Sixties*, 149.

60 Miller, *Democracy Is in the Streets*, 204.

61 Quoted in Breines, *Community and Organization*, 142.

62 Quoted in Miller, *Democracy Is in the Streets*, 215. Compare Berkeley Free Speech activist Jackie Goldberg: "boring, disgusting, time-consuming democracy." Interviewed in the film, *Berkeley in the Sixties*.

63 Letter from Evan Metcalf, *ERAP Newsletter*, July 23, 1965, quoted in Breines, *Community and Organization*, 148.

64 Quoted in *Community and Organization*, 148–9.

65 Quoted in Breines, *Community and Organization*, 143. See also Evans, *Personal Politics*, 141.

66 Quoted in Miller, *Democracy Is in the Streets*, 206.

67 Quoted in Evans, *Personal Politics*, 136.

68 Quoted in Miller, *Democracy Is in the Streets*, 215.

69 Todd Gitlin originated these acronyms, as a joke. Personal communication, Berkeley, CA, June 1992.

70 Richard M. Flacks, *Making History: The American Left and the American Mind* (New York: Columbia University Press, 1988), 163.

71 Hans Koning, quoted in Morgan, *60s Experience*, 20.

72 Quoted in Williams, *Eyes on the Prize*, 241.

73 Quoted in Williams, *Eyes on the Prize*, 243.

Three: *Remembering the Sixties*

1 Taylor Branch, quoted in Alexis Jetter, "Mississippi Learning," *New York Times Magazine*, February 21, 1993, 32.

2 Jetter, "Mississippi Learning," 28.

3 Quoted in Jetter, "Mississippi Learning," 29.

4 "The Living Arts," *New York Times*, March 1, 1991, B1.

5 John Morton Blum, *Years of Discord: American Politics and Society, 1961–1974* (New York: W.W. Norton, 1991).

6 Peter Collier and David Horowitz, eds., *Second Thoughts: Former Radicals Look Back at the Sixties* (Lanham, MD: Madison Books, 1989), xii.

7 Peter Collier and David Horowitz, *Destructive Generation: Second Thoughts About the Sixties* (New York: Summit Books, 1989), 252; Peter Collier, "Foreward," in Collier and Horowitz, *Second Thoughts*, xv.

8 Allan Bloom, *The Closing of the American Mind* (New York: Simon and Schuster, 1987), 314.

9 Michael Barone, *Our Country: The Shaping of America from Roosevelt to Reagan* (New York: Free Press, Macmillan Inc., 1990), 385.

10 Barone, *Our Country*, 670.

11 P.J. O'Rourke, "The Awful Power of Make Believe," in Collier and Horowitz, *Second Thoughts*, 208.

12 Collier and Horowitz, *Destructive Generation*, 244.

13 Irving Kristol, in "Second Thoughts: A Generational Perspective," in Collier and Horowitz, *Second Thoughts*, 186.

14 Kimball, *Tenured Radicals*, xv.

15 Collier, "Foreword," xiv; Carol Iannone, "The Feminist Confusion," 153; Novak, "Humble Wisdom," 237; Loury, "Black Political Culture," 147, all in Collier and Horowitz, *Second Thoughts*. D'Souza titles a chapter, "Profiles in Cowardice," in *Illiberal Education*.

16 Harris Wofford, "What Kennedys and King can teach us in the 90s," *Philadelphia Inquirer*, November 22, 1992.

17 Wofford, "Kennedys and King."

18 Jackie Goldberg, in the film *Berkeley in the Sixties*, 1990.

19 Breines, *Community and Organization*, xv–xvi.

20 Miller, *Democracy Is in the Streets*, 327.

21 Gitlin, *The Sixties*, 3.

22 Breines, *Community and Organization*, xiv.

23 Breines, *Community and Organization*, 6–7.

24 David Farber, *Chicago '68*, 223.

25 Barbara Epstein, *Political Protest and Cultural Revolution: Nonviolent Direct Action in the 1970s and 1980s* (Berkeley: University of California Press, 1991), 21–22.

26 Gitlin, *Sixties*, 4.

27 Burns, *Social Movements of the 1960s*, 4, 135.

28 Hayden, *Reunion*, 505.

29 Mary King, *Freedom Song*, 297.

30 Sale, *SDS*, 5–6.

31 Farber, *Chicago '68*, 245.

32 Elizabeth Larson, "Youth Environmental Movement Flowers," *Utne Reader* (March/April 1991), 31. Similarly, an article on the influence of the sixties on political activity at the University of Texas accentuates the negative: "Yet Ms Luckett says her revolution will be different from the late 60's. 'We have learned from what students did 20 years ago,' she said, 'and hopefully we are a bit more disciplined and have a better understanding of how the power structure works.'" Roberto Suro, "Austin Journal: Outlook of the 60's On Issues Of the 90's," *New York Times*, May 7, 1990.

33 Camille Paglia, "A Scholar and a Not-So-Gentle Woman," *Philadelphia Inquirer IMAGE*, July 7, 1991.

34 Miller, *Democracy Is in the Streets*, 327.

35 Hayden, *Reunion*, xvi.

36 Quoted in Lucinda Franks, "Annals of Crime: Return of the Fugitive, *The New Yorker* (June 13, 1994), 42.

37 President George Bush, Inaugural Address, January 1988, reprinted in Gerald Pomper et al, eds., *The Election of 1988: Reports and Interpretations* (Chatham, NJ: Chatham House, 1989), 210.

38 Quoted in Dowd, "War Introduces Nation."

39 Gross, "Vietnam Generation."

40 Peter Applebome, "The Antiwar Movement: Protestors Face Conflicts in Their Ranks as They Try to Gain Momentum," *New York Times*, January 21, 1991.

41 Peter Applebome, "A Year After Victory, Joy Is A Ghost," *New York Times*, January 16, 1992. Richard Barnet offers a representative sampling of "jeremiads since the war," in "Reflections: The Disorders of Peace," *The New Yorker*, January 20, 1992.

42 B. Drummond Ayres Jr., "Solemn Roll-Call Floats Over Vietnam Memorial," *New York Times*, November 11, 1992.

43 Thomas L. Friedman, "Clinton, in Vietnam War Tribute, Finds Old Wound Is Slow to Heal," *New York Times*, June 1, 1993.

44 On Clinton and the draft, see Elizabeth Becker, "Vietnam Again Haunts Politics," and R. W. Apple, Jr., "The 60's: Clinton's Views of Draft Reopen a War's Wounds." *New York Times*, February 14, 1992.

45 Frank Rich, "Journal: The Jackie Mystery," *New York Times*, May 26, 1994.

46 R. W. Apple Jr., "Last Farewell to Jacqueline Kennedy Onassis," *New York Times*, May 24, 1994.

47 B. Drummond Ayres Jr., "Wistful Pride and Cynicism Color Americans' Memories of Apollo 11," *New York Times*, July 18, 1994.

48 R.W. Apple, Jr., "Nixon Funeral Becomes a Rite of Reconciliation," *New York Times*, April 28, 1994. Throughout his life, Nixon himself was a genius at convincing Americans to forget his past (this may have been one of his attractions to Clinton, who has quite a bit of

personal history that he would like his fellow citizens to forget).

49 "An open letter to President Bush," *New York Times*, January 8, 1992.

50 Quoted in Wines, "White House Links Riots To Welfare."

51 David E. Rosenbaum, "Political Memo: White House Speaking In Code on Riot's Cause," *New York Times*, May 6, 1992.

52 Quoted in Rosenthal, "Quayle Says Riots Arose," *New York Times*, May 20, 1992.

53 Quoted in Jason DeParle, "In Command: General Says Infantry's Training Will Help It Quickly Restore Calm," *New York Times*, May 3, 1992.

54 Quoted in DeParle, "In Command."

55 Quoted in Jason DeParle, "The Civil Rights Battle Was Easy Next to the Problems of the Ghetto," *New York Times*, May 17, 1992.

Four: *"Is This America?"*

1 Quoted in Williams, *Eyes on the Prize*, 241.

2 On the founding, see Merrill Jensen, "The Myth of the Critical Period," in Nicholas Cords and Patrick Gerster, eds., *Myth and the American Experience*, Vol. One (Beverly Hills, CA: Glencoe Press, 1973), 124, 126; Bernard Bailyn, *Ideological Origins of the American Revolution* (Cambridge, MA: Harvard University Press, 1967); Gordon S. Wood, *The Creation of the American Republic* (Chapel Hill: University of North Carolina Press, 1969; and J. G. A. Pocock, *The Machiavellian Moment: Florentine Political Thought and the Atlantic Tradition* (Princeton: Princeton University Press, 1975).

3 See Herbert J. Storing, *What the Anti-Federalists Were For: The Political Thought of the Opponents of the Constitution* (Chicago: University of Chicago Press, 1981).

4 James Madison, "Federalist #51," in Alexander Hamilton, James Madison, and John Jay, *The Federalist Papers*, ed. Clinton Rossiter (New York: A Mentor Book, The New American Library, 1961), 323.

5 James Madison, "Federalist #51," 322.

6 The noted political scientist, Richard Neustadt, has described this constitutional principle as "a government of separated institutions *sharing* powers." Richard E. Neustadt, *Presidential Power: The*

Politics of Leadership From FDR to Carter (New York: Macmillan, 1980), 24.

7   Madison, "Federalist #10," in Hamilton, Madison, and Jay, *Federalist Papers*, 78, 83.

8   Pocock, *Machiavellian Moment*, 524. See also Wilson Carey McWilliams, "Democracy and the Citizen: Community, Dignity, and the Crisis of Contemporary Politics in America," in Robert A. Goldwin and William A. Schambra, eds., *How Democratic is the Constitution?* (Washington, DC: American Enterprise Institute for Public Policy Research, 1980); and Sheldon S. Wolin, "E Pluribus Unum," in *The Presence of the Past: Essays on the State and the Constitution* (Baltimore: The Johns Hopkins University Press, 1989).

9   For instance, Michael Parenti contends that "the intent of the framers of the Constitution was to contain democracy, rather than give it free rein, and dilute the democratic will, rather than mobilize it." Michael Parenti, "The Constitution as an Elitist Document," in Julius Lobel, ed., *A Less Than Perfect Union: Alternative Perspectives on the U.S. Constitution* (New York: Monthly Review Press, 1988), 39.

10 Madison, "Federalist #10," 79, 84. See also Joshua Miller, *The Rise and Fall of Democracy in Early America, 1630–1789* (University Park, PA: Pennsylvania State University Press, 1991); and Jesse Lemisch, "The American Revolution Seen From the Bottom Up," in Barton J. Bernstein, ed., *Towards A New Past: Dissenting Essays in American History* (New York: Pantheon Books, Random House, 1968), 17.

11 Melancton Smith, in Storing, *Anti-Federalists*, 19.

12 Impartial Examiner, in Storing, *Anti-Federalists*, 75.

13 Hannah Arendt, *On Revolution* (New York: Penguin Books, 1986), 232.

14 In Michael Lienesch's formulation, the founders were "constitutional psychologists...determined to create a psychology to perpetuate their government," *New Order of the Ages: Time, the Constitution, and the Making Of Modern American Political Thought* (Princeton: Princeton University Press, 1988), 182.

15 Alexis de Tocqueville, *Democracy in America*, trans. George Lawrence, ed. J.P. Mayer (New York: Perennial Library, Harper & Row, 1969), 68–70, 513–17, 503–06, 316–340.

16 Tocqueville, *Democracy in America*, 691–2.

17 Tocqueville, *Democracy in America*, 513, 510–11.

18 Evans and Boyte, *Free Spaces* 17, 18.

19 For general accounts of these incidents and suggestions for further reading on American movements, see Evans and Boyte, *Free Spaces*; on the Lowell strike and the women's suffrage movement; see Thomas R. Brooks, *Toil and Trouble: A History of American Labor* (New York: Dell Publishing, 1964); and on labor, see Mike Davis, *Prisoners of the American Dream: Politics and the Economy in the History of the US Working Class* (London: Verso, 1986); on the socialists, see Flacks, *Making History*.

20 Lawrence Goodwyn, *Populist Moment*.

21 Quoted in Goodwyn, *Populist Moment*, xix.

22 Flacks, *Making History*, 106.

23 Goodwyn, *Populist Moment*, xiii, xix.

24 Goodwyn *Populist Moment*, 297.

25 Brooks, *Toil and Trouble*, 128–30.

26 On this strike, see Brooks, *Toil and Trouble*, 183–85, and Saul D. Alinsky, *John L. Lewis: An Unauthorized Biography* (New York: Vintage Books, 1970), 97–147.

27 See Peter Rachleff, "Seeds of a Labor Insurgency," *The Nation*, February 21, 1994, 226.

28 See Isserman, *If I Had a Hammer*. Sharon Jeffrey was a red diaper baby.

29 R. W. B. Lewis, *The American Adam: Innocence, Tragedy, and Tradition in the Nineteenth Century* (Chicago: University of Chicago Press, 1955), 1.

30 Louis Hartz, *The Liberal Tradition in America* (New York: Harcourt, Brace, and World, 1955), 20. See also Daniel J. Boorstin, *The Genius of American Politics* (Chicago: University of Chicago Press, 1953); Richard Hofstadter, *The American Political Tradition* (New York: Vintage Books, 1948); and David M. Potter, *People of Plenty: Economic Abundance and the American Character* (Chicago: Phoenix Books, University of Chicago Press, 1954).

31 Perry Miller, *Nature's Nation* (Cambridge, MA: Belknap Press, 1967), 3.

32 Slotkin, *The Fatal Environment*, 32. See also the other two volumes of Slotkin's excellent triology: *Regeneration Through Violence: The Mythology of the American Frontier, 1600–1860* (Middleton: Wesleyan University Press, 1986); and *Gunfighter Nation: The Myth of the Frontier in the Twentieth Century* (New York: Atheneum, 1992).

33 Perry Miller, *Errand into the Wilderness* (New York: Harper & Row, Harper Torchbooks, 1964) 1–15.

34 John Winthrop, "A Modell of Christian Charity," in Perry Miller and Thomas H. Johnson, eds., *The Puritans: A Sourcebook of Their Writings*, Vol. One (New York: Harper Torchbooks, 1963), 199.

35 Slotkin, *Regeneration Through Violence*, 22.

36 Sacvan Bercovitch, *The American Jeremiad* (Madison: University of Wisconsin Press, 1978), 177.

37 Michael Paul Rogin, *Ronald Reagan, The Movie and Other Episodes in Political Demonology*, (Berkeley: University of California Press, 1987), 107.

38 Slotkin, *The Fatal Environment*, 32, 47.

39 Woodrow Wilson, "Declaration of War," in Michael B. Levy, *Political Thought in America: An Anthology*, 2nd ed. (Prospect Heights, IL: Waveland Press, 1988), 521.

40 Rogin, *Ronald Reagan*, 68.

41 Quoted in Burr Snider, "Veterans of war pledge allegiance to peace," *San Francisco Examiner*, May 19, 1991.

42 John H. Schaar, "The Case for Patriotism," in *Legitimacy in the Modern State* (New Brunswick: Transaction Press, 1981), 291, 293. Compare Robert N. Bellah, *The Broken Covenant: American Civil Religion in Time of Trial* (New York: Seabury, 1975).

43 "The Declaration of Independence," in Levy, *Political Thought*, 83.

44 Abraham Lincoln, *His Speeches and Writings* (New York: The Universal Library, 1962), 401.

45 Lincoln, *His Speeches and Writings*, 403.

46 Lincoln, *His Speeches and Writings*, 734.

47 Abraham Lincoln, *The Political Thought of Abraham Lincoln*, ed. Richard N. Current (Indianapolis: Bobbs-Merrill, 1967), 105, 207–213.

48 Flacks, *Making History*, 189.

48 Martin Luther King, Jr., "Letter from a Birmingham Jail," 94. Passage is quoted in full Ch. two above.

50 James M. Lawson, Jr., "From a Lunch-Counter Stool," 314.

51 SDS, "The Port Huron Statement," in Albert and Albert, *The Sixties Papers*, 176.

52 See Miller on authenticity and existentialism in SDS. *"Democracy Is in the streets,"* 145–47, 204.

53 Quoted in Powledge, *Free At Last?*, 547.

54 Quoted in Mary King, *Freedom Song*, 504.

55 Bercovitch, *The American Jeremaid*, 180.

56 Quoted in Young, *Vietnam Wars*.

Conclusion: *Reclaiming Democracy*

1 Interviews with Zulene Mayfield, chairperson of Chester Residents Concerned for Quality Living, March 12 and 16, 1995. See also Hal Ellis, "'Environmental Racism," *Delaware County Daily Times*, October 1, 1993; Dan Hardy, "Silence Golden on Street That was Living Hell," *Philadelphia Inquirer*, June 27, 1993; Joe Hart, "Marchers trash Westy," *Delaware County Daily Times*, April 6, 1993.

2 See Barton Smith, "Political Organizing and Empowerment in Chester," unpublished thesis, Department of Political Science, Swarthmore College, 1992.

3 Interview with Zulene Mayfield, March 16, 1995.

BIBLIOGRAPHY

Albert, Judith and Stewart Albert. Eds. *The Sixties Papers: Documents of a Rebellious Decade*. New York: Praeger Publishers, 1984.

Alinsky, Saul D. *John L. Lewis: An Unauthorized Biography*. New York: Vintage Books, 1970.

Anderson, Dwight G. *Abraham Lincoln: The Quest for Immortality*. New York: Alfred A. Knopf, 1982.

Arblaster, Anthony. *Democracy*. Minneapolis: University of Minnesota Press, 1987.

Arendt, Hannah. *Between Past and Future: Eight Exercises in Political Thought*. New and enl. ed., New York: The Viking Press, 1968.

———. *Crises of the Republic*. New York: A Harvest/HBJ Book, Harcourt Brace Jovanovich, 1972.

———. *Eichmann in Jerusalem: A Report on the Banality of Evil*. Rev. and enl. ed. New York: Penguin Books, 1984.

———. *The Human Condition*. Garden City, NY: Doubleday Anchor Books, 1959.

———. *Men in Dark Times*. San Diego: A Harvest/HBJ Book, Harcourt Brace Jovanovich, 1968.

———. *On Revolution*. New York: Penguin Books, 1987.

———. *The Origins of Totalitarianism*. Cleveland: Meridian Books, The World Publishing Co., 1962.

———. "Personal Responsibility Under Dictatorship." *Listener* 72 (August 6, 1964): 185–7, 205.

———. "Reflections on Little Rock." *Dissent* (Winter 1959), 45–56.

Aristotle. *The Politics of Aristotle*. Ed. and trans. Ernest Barker. London: Oxford University Press, 1971.

Bailyn, Bernard. *Ideological Origins of the American Revolution*. Cambridge, MA: Harvard University Press, 1967.

Baldwin, James. *The Fire Next Time*. New York: A Dell Book, 1963.

Ball, Terence and James Farr and Russell L. Hanson. Eds. *Political Innovation and Conceptual Change*. Cambridge: Cambridge University Press, 1989.

Barber, Benjamin. *Strong Democracy: Participatory Politics for a New Age*. Berkeley: University of California Press, 1984.

Barone, Michael. *Our Country: The Shaping of American from Roosevelt to Reagan*. New York: The Free Press, Macmillan Inc., 1990.

Bellah, Robert N., et al. *Habits of the Heart: Individualism and Commitment in American Life*. New York: Perennial Library, Harper & Row, 1986.

Bercovitch, Sacvan. *The American Jeremiad*. Madison: University of Wisconsin Press, 1978.

Berelson, Bernard R., and Paul F. Lazarsfeld and William N. McPhee. *Voting*. Chicago: University of Chicago Press, 1954.

Berman, Paul. Ed. *Debating P.C.: The Controversy Over Political Correctness on College Campuses*. New York: Laurel, Dell Publishing, 1992.

Bloom, Allan. *The Closing of the American Mind*. New York: Simon and Schuster, 1987.

Blum, John Morton. *Years of Discord: American Politics and Society, 1961–1974*. New York: W.W. Norton, 1991.

Boorstin, Daniel J. *The Genius of American Politics*. Chicago: University of Chicago Press, 1953.

Boyte, Harry C. *The Backyard Revolution: Understanding the New Citizen Movement*. Philadelphia: Temple University Press, 1980.

———. *CommonWealth: A Return to Citizen Politics*. New York: Free Press, 1989.

———. *The New Populism: The Politics of Empowerment*. Philadelphia: Temple University Press, 1986.

Branch, Taylor. *Parting the Waters: America in the King Years, 1954–63*. New York: Simon and Schuster, 1988.

Breines, Wini. *Community and Organization in the New Left, 1962–1968: The Great Refusal*. 2nd ed. New Brunswick: Rutgers University Press, 1989.

Brooks, Thomas. *Toil and Trouble: A History of American Labor* New York: Dell Publishing, 1964.

Buber, Martin. *The Prophetic Faith*. New York: Harper Torchbooks, Harper & Row, 1960.

Burnheim, John. *Is Democracy Possible? The Alternative to Electoral Politics.* Berkeley: University of California Press, 1985.

Burns, Stewart. *Social Movements of the 1960s: Searching for Democracy.* Boston: Twayne Publishers, 1990.

Calvert, Gregory Navala. *Democracy From the Heart: Spiritual Values, Decentralism, and Democratic Idealism in the Movement of the Sixties.* Eugene, OR: Communitas Press, 1991.

Carson, Clayborne. *In Struggle: SNNC and the Black Awakening of the 1960s.* Cambridge, MA: Harvard University Press, 1981.

Caute, David. *The Year of the Barricades: A Journey Through 1968.* New York: Perennial Library, Harper & Row, 1988.

Cockburn, Alexander. "Beat the Devil." *The Nation* (May 27, 1991): 690–692, 704–705.

———. "Cockburn Replies." *The Nation* (March 9, 1992): 319–320.

Cohen, Joshua, and Joel Rogers. *On Democracy: Toward a Transformation of American Society.* New York: Penguin Books, 1986.

Cohen, Mitchell, and Dennis Hale. Eds. *The New Student Left.* Rev. ed. Boston: Beacon Press, 1967.

Collier, Peter, and David Horowitz. *Destructive Generation: Second Thoughts About the Sixties.* New York: Summit Books, 1989.

Collier, Peter, and David Horowitz. Eds. *Second Thoughts: Former Radicals Look Back at the Sixties.* Lanham, MD: Madison Books, 1989.

Connolly, William E. *The Terms of Discourse.* 2d ed. Ann Arbor: Edwards Bros., 1983.

Cook, Terrence E., and Patrick M. Morgan. Eds. *Participatory Democracy.* New York: Harper & Row, 1971.

Cords, Nicholas, and Patrick Gerster. Eds. *Myth and the American Experience.* Two vols. Beverly Hills, CA: Glencoe Press, 1973.

D'Souza, Dinesh. *Illiberal Education: The Politics of Race and Gender on Campus.* New York: Free Press, Macmillan, Inc., 1991.

Dahl, Robert A. *After the Revolution?* New Haven: Yale University Press, 1970.

———. *Democracy and Its Critics.* New Haven: Yale University Press, 1989.

———. *A Preface to Democratic Theory.* Chicago: Phoenix Books, University of Chicago Press, 1967.

Dahl, Robert A., and Edward R. Tufte. *Size and Democracy*. Stanford, CA: Standford University Press, 1973.

Darnton, Nina. "Lifestyle: Not-So-Groovy Threads." *Newsweek* (March 25, 1991): 63.

Davis, Mike. *Prisoners of the American Dream: Politics and Economy in the History of the US Working Class*. London: Verso Press, 1986.

Davis, Natalie Zemon, and Richard Starn. "Introduction" to "Special Issue: Memory and Counter–Memory." *representations* 26 (Spring 1989): 1–6.

De Tocqueville, Alexis. *Democracy in America*. Trans. George Lawrence, ed. J. P. Mayer. New York: Perennial Library, Harper & Row, 1988.

———. *The Old Regime and the French Revolution*. Trans. Stuart Gilbert. New York: Doubleday Anchor, 1955.

———. *Recollections*. Trans. George Lawrence, Eds. J.P. Mayer and A.P. Kerr. Garden City, NY: Doubleday.

Didion, Joan. *The White Album*. New York: Pocket Books, 1980.

Dietz, Mary G. "Patriotism." In Terence Ball, James Farr, and Russell L. Hanson. Eds. *Political Innovation and Conceptual Change*. Cambridge: Cambridge University Press, 1989.

———. "Populism, Patriotism, and the Need for Roots." In Harry C. Boyte and Frank Reissman, *The New Populism: The Politics of Empowerment*. Philadelphia: Temple University Press, 1986.

Dinnerstein, Dorothy. *The Mermaid and the Minotaur: Sexual Arrangements and Human Malaise*. New York: Harper Colophon Books, 1977.

Dittmar, Linda, and Gene Marchand. Eds. *From Hanoi to Hollywood: The Vietnam War in American Film*. New Brunswick: Rutgers University Press, 1990.

Duncan, Graeme. Ed. *Democratic Theory and Practice*. Cambridge: Cambridge University Press, 1983.

Epstein, Barbara. *Political Protest and Cultural Revolution: Nonviolent Direct Action in the 1970s and 1980s*. Berkeley: University of California Press, 1991.

Evans, Sara M. *Personal Politics: The Roots of Women's Liberation in the Civil Rights Movement and the New Left*. New York: Vintage Books, 1980.

Evans, Sara M., and Harry C. Boyte. *Free Spaces: The Sources of Democratic*

Change in America. New York: Perennial Library, Harper & Row, 1986.

Farber, David. *Chicago '68*. Chicago: University of Chicago Press, 1988.

Flacks, Richard. *Making History: The American Left and the American Mind*. New York: Columbia University Press, 1988.

———. "Making History vs. Making Life: Dilemmas of an American Left." *Sociological Inquiry* 46 (1976): 263–80.

Flacks, Richard, and Jack Whalen. *Beyond the Barricades: The Sixties Generation Grows Up*. Philadelphia: Temple University Press, 1989.

Franke, Lucinda. "Annals of Crime: Return of the Fugitive." *The New Yorker* (June 13, 1994): 40–59.

Fraser, Ronald. *1968: A Student Generation in Revolt*. New York: Pantheon Books, 1988.

Gamson, William A. *The Strategy of Social Protest*. Homewood, IL: The Dorsey Press, 1975.

Gaventa, John. *Power and Powerlessness: Quiescence and Rebellion in an Appalachian Valley*. Urbana, IL: University of Illinois Press, 1980.

Geertz, Clifford. *The Interpretation of Cultures*. New York: Basic Books, 1973.

Geoghegan, Thomas. *Which Side Are You On? Trying to Be for Labor When It's Flat on Its Back*. New York: Farrar, Strauss & Giroux, 1991.

Gitlin, Todd. *The Sixties: Years of Hope, Days of Rage*. New York: Bantam Books, 1987.

———. *The Whole World is Watching: Mass Media in the Making and Unmaking of the New Left*. Berkeley: University of California Press, 1980.

Goodwyn, Lawrence. "Organizing Democracy," *Democracy* (January 1981): 41–60.

———. *The Populist Moment: A Short History of the Agrarian Revolt in America*. New York: Oxford University Press, 1978.

Gould, Carol C. *Rethinking Democracy: Freedom and Social Cooperation in Politics, Economy, and Society*. Cambridge: Cambridge University Press, 1990.

Green, Philip. Ed. *Democracy*. New Jersey: Humanities Press, 1993.

———. *Retrieving Democracy: In Search of Civic Equality*. Totowa, NJ: Rowman and Allanheld, 1985.

Green, Philip, and Sanford Levinson. Eds. *Power and Community: Dissenting Essays in Political Science*. New York: Vintage Books, 1970.

Greene, Melissa Fay. *Praying for Sheetrock: A Work of Nonfiction*. Reading, MA: Addison-Wesley Publishing Company, 1991.

Greider, William S. *Who Will Tell the People: The Betrayal of American Democracy*. New York: Simon and Schuster, 1992.

Hallin, Daniel C. *The "Uncensored War": The Media and Vietnam*. New York: Oxford University Press, 1986.

Hampsher-Monk, Iain. "The historical study of 'democracy.'" In Graeme Duncan. Ed. *Democratic Theory and Practice*. Cambridge: Cambridge University Press, 1983.

Hampton, Henry, and Steve Fayer, with Karen Flynn. *Voices of Freedom: An Oral History of the Civil Rights Movement from the 1950s through the 1980s*. New York: Bantam Books, 1991.

Hanson, Russell L. "Democracy." In Terence Ball, James Farr, and Russell L. Hanson. Eds. *Political Innovation and Conceptual Change*. Cambridge University Press, 1989.

———. *The Democratic Imagination in America: Conversations with Our Past*. Princeton: Princeton University Press, 1985.

Hartz, Louis. *The Liberal Tradition in America*. New York: Harcourt, Brace, and World, 1955.

Heaney, Seamus. *The Cure At Troy: A Version of Sophocles's Philoctetes*. London: Faber and Faber, in association with Field Day, 1990.

Hofstadter, Richard. *The American Political Tradition*. New York: Vintage Books, 1948.

Howard, Gerald. Ed. *The Sixties: Arts, Politics, and Media of our Most Explosive Decade*. 2d ed. New York: Paragon House, 1991.

Huntington, Samuel P. "Chapter III—The United States." In Michel J. Crozier, Samuel P. Huntington, and Joji Watanuki. Eds. *The Crisis of Democracy: Report on the Governability of Democracies to the Trilateral Commission*. New York: New York University Press, 1975.

Ignatieff, Michael. *The Needs of Strangers: An Essay on Privacy, Solidarity, and the Politics of Being Human*. New York: Penguin Books, 1984.

Isserman, Maurice. *If I Had a Hammer: The Death of the Old Left and the Birth of the New Left*. New York: Basic Books, 1987.

Jacobs, Paul and Saul Landau. Eds. *The New Radicals: A Report With Documents*. New York: Vintage Books, 1966.

Jacobson, Norman. "Political Science and Political Education." *The American Political Science Review* LVII (September 1963): 561–69.

Jensen, Merrill. "The Myth of the Critical Period." In Nicholas Cords and Patrick Gerster. Eds. *Myth and the American Experience*. Vol. I. Beverly Hills, CA: Glencoe Press, 1973.

Katsiaficas, George. *The Imagination of the New Left: A Global Analysis of 1968*. Boston: South End Press, 1987.

Kemmis, Daniel. *Community and the Politics of Place*. Norman, OK: University of Oklahoma Press, 1990.

Kimball, Roger. *Tenured Radicals: How Politics Has Corrupted Our Higher Education*. New York: Harper & Row, 1990.

King, Jr., Martin Luther. "Letter From A Birmingham Jail." In *Why We Can't Wait*. New York: The New American Library, 1964.

King, Mary. *Freedom Song: A Personal Story of the 1960s Civil Rights Movement*. New York: Quill, William Morrow, 1987.

Kohr, Leopold. *The Breakdown of Nations*. New York: Routledge & Kegan Paul, 1986.

Koning, Hans. *Nineteen Sixty-Eight: A Personal Report*. New York: Norton, 1987.

Larson, Elizabeth. "Youth Environmental Movement Flowers." *Utne Reader* (March/April 1991): 30–31.

Lawrence, D.H. *Studies in Classic American Literature*. New York: The Viking Press, 1969.

Lemisch, Jesse. "The American Revolution Seen From the Bottom Up." In Barton J. Bernstein, ed., *Towards A New Past: Dissenting Essays in American History*. New York: Pantheon Books, Random House, 1968.

Levy, Michael B. Ed. *Political Thought in America: An Anthology*. 2nd Ed. Prospect Height IL: Waveland Press; 1988.

Lewis, R. W. B. *The American Adam: Innocence, Tragedy, and Tradition in the Nineteenth Century*. Chicago: University of Chicago Press, 1955.

Lienesch, Michael. *New Order of the Ages: Time, the Constitution, and the Making Of Modern American Political Thought*. Princeton: Princeton University Press, 1988.

Lincoln, Abraham. *His Speeches and Writings*. New York: The Universal Library, 1962.

———. *The Political Thought of Abraham Lincoln*. Ed. Richard N. Current. Indianapolis: The Bobbs-Merrill Company, 1967.

Lorde, Audre. "Learning From the Sixties." In *Sister Outsider: Essays and Speeches*. Trumansburg, New York: The Crossing Press, 1984.

Lucas, J. R. *Democracy and Participation*. London: Penguin Books, 1976.

Lummis, Charles Douglas. "The Radicalism of Democracy." *Democracy* 2 (Fall 1982): 9–16.

Machiavelli, Niccolo. *The Prince and the Discourses*. New York: The Modern Library, Random House, 1950.

Macpherson, C. B. *Democratic Theory: Essays in Retrieval*. Oxford: Clarendon Press, 1971.

———. *The Real World of Democracy: The Massey Lectures*. Oxford: Oxford University Press, 1971.

Madison, James, and Alexander Hamilton and John Jay. *The Federalist Papers*. Ed. Clinton Rossiter. New York: A Mentor Book, The New American Library, 1961.

Mailer, Norman. *The Armies of the Night*. New York: Signet Books, 1968.

Mansbridge, Jane. *Beyond Adversary Democracy*. 2d ed. Chicago: University of Chicago Press, 1983.

Marable, Manning. *Race, Reform, and Rebellion: The Second Reconstruction in Black America, 1945–1990*. Jackson: University of Mississippi Press, 1991.

Margolis, Michael. "Democracy: American style." In Graeme Duncan. Ed. *Democratic Theory and Practice*. Cambridge: Cambridge University Press 1983.

Marx, Karl. "The Eighteenth Brumaire of Louis Bonaparte." In Robert C. Tucker. Ed. *The Marx-Engels Reader*. New York: W. W. Norton and Company, 1978.

McAdam, Doug. *Political Process and the Development of Black Insurgency, 1930–1970*. Chicago: University of Chicago Press, 1982.

McWilliams, Wilson Carey. "Democracy and the Citizen: Community, Dignity, and the Crisis of Contemporary Politics in America." In Robert A. Goldwin and William A. Schambra. Eds. *How Democratic is the Constitution?* Washington, D.C: American Enterprise Institute for Public Policy Research, 1980.

Meier, August, and Elliott Rudwick and Francis L. Broderick. Eds. *Black Protest Thought in the Twentieth Century*. 2d ed. Indianapolis: Bobbs-Merrill, 1971.

Mendel-Reyes, Meta. "Remembering Cesar." *Radical History Review* 58 (Winter 1994): 142–50.

Michels, Robert. *Political Parties: A Sociological Study of the Oligarchical Tendencies of Modern Democracy*. Glencoe, IL: Free Press, 1949.

Milgram, Stanley. *Obedience to Authority: An Experimental View*. New York: Harper Torchbooks, 1974.

Mill, John Stuart. *Considerations on Representative Government*. Chicago: Gateway Edition, Henry Regnery Company, 1962.

———. "On Liberty." In Max Lerner. Ed. *Essential Works of John Stuart Mill*. New York: Bantam Books, 1965.

Miller, James. *"Democracy Is in the Streets": From Port Huron to the Siege of Chicago*. New York: Simon and Schuster, 1987.

Miller, Joshua. *The Rise and Fall of Democracy in Early America, 1630–1789*. University Park, PA: Pennsylvania State University Press, 1991.

Miller, Perry. *Errand Into the Wilderness*. New York: Harper Torchbooks, Harper & Row, 1964.

———. *Nature's Nation*. Cambridge, MA: Belknap Press, 1967.

Miller, Perry and Thomas Johnson. Eds. *The Puritans: A Sourcebook of Their Writings*. Vol. One. New York: Harper Torchbooks, 1963.

Mills, C. Wright. *The Sociological Imagination*. New York: Oxford University Press, 1959.

Moody, Anne. *Coming of Age in Mississippi*. New York: A Laurel Book, Dell Publishing, 1968.

Morgan, Edward P. *The 60s Experience: Hard Lessons About Modern America*. Philadelphia: Temple University Press, 1991.

Morris, Aldon D. *The Origins of the Civil Rights Movement: Black Communities Organizing for Change*. New York: The Free Press, 1984.

Nora, Pierre. "Between Memory and History: Les Lieux de Memoire." *Representations* 26 (Spring 1989): 7–25.

Oates, Marylouise. *Making Peace*. New York: Warner Books, 1991.

Palmer, R.R. "Notes on the Use of the Word, 'Democracy,' 1789–1799." *Political Science Quarterly* 48 (June 1953): 203–26.

Parenti, Michael. "The Constitution as an Elitist Document." In Julius Lobel. Ed. *A Less Than Perfect Union: Alternative Perspectives on the U.S. Constitution.* New York: Monthly Review Press, 1988.

Pateman, Carole. *Participation and Democratic Theory.* Cambridge: Cambridge University Press, 1970.

Paxton, Robert O. "Tricks of Memory." Review of *The Vichy Syndrome,* by Henry Rousso. *The New York Review of Books.* November 7, 1991: 51–52.

Percy, Walker. "Metaphor As Mistake." *The Sewanee Review* LXVI (January 3, 1958): 79–99.

Phillips, Anne. *Engendering Democracy.* University Park, PA: The Pennsylvania State University Press, 1991.

Pitkin, Hannah Fenichel. *Fortune Is a Woman: Gender and Politics in the Thought of Niccolo Machiavelli.* Berkeley: University of California Press, 1984.

———. "Justice: On Relating Private and Public." *Political Theory* 9 (August 1981): 327–52.

———. Rethinking Reification." *Theory and Society* 16 (1987): 263–94.

———. *Wittgenstein and Justice: On the Significance of Ludwig Wittgenstein for Social and Political Thought.* Berkeley: University of California Press, 1972.

Pitkin, Hanna Fenichel, and Sara Shumer. "On Participation." *Democracy* 2 (Fall 1982): 43–54.

Piven, Frances Fox, and Richard A. Cloward. *Poor People's Movements: Why They Succeed, How They Fail.* New York: Vintage Books, 1979.

Pocock, J. G. A. *The Machiavellian Moment: Florentine Political Thought and the Atlantic Tradition.* Princeton: Princeton University Press, 1975.

Potter, David M. *People of Plenty: Economic Abundance and the American Character.* Chicago: Phoenix Books, University of Chicago Press, 1954.

Powledge, Fred. *Free At Last? The Civil Rights Movement and the People Who Made it.* Boston: Little, Brown, 1991.

Pynchon, Thomas. *Vineland.* Boston: Little, Brown and Co., 1990.

Rachleff, Peter. "Seeds of a Labor Insurgency." *The Nation* (February 21, 1994): 226–29.

Raines, Howell. *My Soul Is Rested: Movement Days in the Deep South Remembered.* New York: Penguin Books, 1987.

Rodgers, Daniel T. *Contested Truths: Keywords in American Politics Since Independence*. New York: Basic Books, 1987.

Rogin, Michael Paul. "In Defense of the New Left." *Democracy* 3 (Fall 1983): 106–16.

——. "JFK: The Movie." *The American Historical Review* 97 (April 1992): 500–05.

——. "'Make My Day!' Spectacle as Amnesia in Imperial Politics." *Representations* 29 (Winter 1990): 99–123.

——. *Ronald Reagan, the Movie and other Episodes in Political Demonology*. Berkeley: University of California Press, 1987.

Rousseau, Jean Jacques. *The Social Contract*. Trans. Charles Frankel. New York: Hafner Publishing Company, 1947.

Rousso, Henry. *The Vichy Syndrome: History and Memory in France since 1944*. Trans. Arthur Goldhammer, from 2d rev. ed. Cambridge, MA: Harvard University Press, 1991.

Rowe, John Carlos, and Rick Berg. Eds. *The Vietnam War and American Culture*. New York: Columbia University Press, 1991.

Sale, Kirkpatrick. *Human Scale*. New York: Coward, McCann, and Geoghegan, 1980.

——. *SDS*. New York: Vintage Books, 1974.

Santoro, Gene. "Music: Rockin' in the Free World." *The Nation* (March 11, 1991): 318.

Sayers, Sohnya, et al. *The 60s Without Apology*. Minneapolis: University of Minnesota Press, in cooperation with *Social Text*, 1984.

Schaar, John H. *Legitimacy in the Modern State*. New Brunswick: Transaction Press, 1981.

——. "Liberty/Authority/Community in the Political Thought of John Winthrop." *Political Theory* 19 (November 1991): 493–518.

Schell, Jonathan. "Introduction." In Adam Michnik, *Letters From Prison and Other Essays*. Berkeley: University of California Press, 1987.

Schumpeter, Joseph A. *Capitalism, Socialism, and Democracy*. 3d ed. New York: Harper Torchbooks, 1976.

Scott, James C. *Weapons of the Weak: Everyday Forms of Peasant Resistance*. New Haven: Yale University Press, 1985.

Silko, Leslie Marmon. *Ceremony*. New York: A Signet Book, New American

Library, 1977.

Singer, Daniel. "Letter From Europe." *The Nation* (June 20, 1994: 863–65.

Slotkin, Richard. *The Fatal Environment: The Myth of the Frontier in the Age of Industrialization, 1800–1890.* Middletown, CT: Wesleyan University Press, 1986.

———. *Gunfighter Nation: The Myth of the Frontier in the Twentieth Century.* New York: Atheneum, 1992.

———. *Regeneration Through Violence: The Mythology of the American Frontier, 1600–1860.* Middletown, CT: Wesleyan University Press, 1973.

Storing, Herbert J. *What the Anti-Federalists Were For: The Political Thought of the Opponents of the Constitution.* Chicago: University of Chicago Press, 1981.

Students for a Democratic Society. "The Port Huron Statement." In Judith Albert and Stewart Albert. *The Sixties Papers: Documents of a Rebellious Decade.* New York: Praeger Publishers, 1984.

Sturken, Marita. "The Wall, the Screen, and the Image: The Vietnam Veterans' Memorial." *Representations* 35 (Summer 1991): 118–42.

Terkel, Studs. *The Great Divide: Second Thoughts on the American Dream.* New York: Avon Books, 1988.

Thoreau, Henry David. "Civil Disobedience." In *Selected Writings.* New York: Appleton-Century-Crofts, 1958.

Verba Sidney, and Norman H. Nie. *Participation in America.* New York: Harper & Row, 1972.

White, Hayden. *Metahistory: The Historical Imagination in Nineteenth-Century Europe.* Baltimore: The Johns Hopkins University Press, 1974.

Will, George F. "Slamming the Doors." *Newsweek.* March 25, 1991–65.

Williams, Juan. *Eyes on the Prize: America's Civil Rights Years, 1954–65.* New York: Penguin Books, 1988.

Williams, Raymond. *Keywords: A Vocabulary of Culture and Society.* New York: Oxford University Press, 1976.

Williams, William Carlos. *In the American Grain.* New York: New Directions Books, 1956.

Winthrop, John. "A Model of Christian Charity." In Perry Miller and Thomas H. Johnson. Eds. *The Puritans: A Sourcebook of their Writings.* Vol. I. New York: Harper Torchbooks, 1963.

Wolf, Naomi. *The Beauty Myth: How Images of Beauty Are Used Against Women*. New York: William Morrow, 1991.

Wolfe, Alan. *Whose Keeper? Social Science and Moral Obligation*. Berkeley: University of California Press, 1989.

Wolin, Sheldon S. *Politics and Vision: Continuity and Innovation in Western Political Thought*. Boston: Little, Brown, and Co., 1960.

———. *The Presence of the Past: Essays on the State and the Constitution*. Baltimore: The Johns Hopkins University Press, 1989.

———. "What Revolutionary Action Means Today." *Democracy* 2 (Fall 1982): 17–28.

Wood, Gordon S. *The Creation of the American Republic*. Chapel Hill: University of North Carolina Press, 1969.

Young, Marilyn B. *The Vietnam Wars 1945–1990*. New York: HarperCollins, 1991.

Young–Bruehl, Elisabeth. *Hannah Arendt: For Love of the World*. New Haven: Yale University Press, 1982.

INDEX

DATE DUE